THE
ARSENAL
MISCELLANY

THE
ARSENAL
MISCELLANY

BY ADAM GOLD

VSP

Vision Sports Publishing
2 Coombe Gardens,
London, SW20 0QU

www.visionsp.co.uk

Published by Vision Sports Publishing. 2007

ISBN 10: 1-905326-28-9
ISBN 13: 978-1905326-28-0

Printed and bound in the UK by
Cromwell Press Ltd, Trowbridge, Wiltshire

Typeset by Palimpsest Book Production Limited,
Grangemouth, Stirlingshire

A CIP catalogue record for this book is
available from the British Library

Foreword
By Frank McLintock

I am delighted to write the introduction to this book about Arsenal. I think the way it is broken up into the club history, profiles of individual players, facts and figures and quirky stories is great and something that all Gunners fans will really enjoy reading.

As a club Arsenal has always had a special atmosphere, although it's quite hard to define. It's always been a very traditional club, with lots of history. When I first played there it was quite unlike any club I had been to. Just going into the ground or the dressing room at Highbury was very grand, it was like going to a lovely hotel. You almost felt like royalty going there. Everything about the place – from the Marble Halls to the dressing rooms and the organization behind the scenes – was absolutely top class.

When I signed from Leicester in 1964 I was very impressed by the surroundings but, unfortunately, the team wasn't particularly good. Back then Arsenal were a sleeping giant and hadn't done a great deal for a long time. That all changed when we eventually won the Fairs Cup in 1970 – our first trophy for 17 years. After we lost the first leg 3-1 to Anderlecht, who were an outstanding team, we knew we would have to play the game of our lives in the return leg at Highbury. With the help of 62,000 fans we did just that to overhaul the deficit. That was a very special night for the club and the players because at last we had won something.

The Fairs Cup victory gave us a bit of belief in ourselves and the platform to go forward. The next season we won the Double for the first time in the club's history, an achievement which I'm pleased to see gets a lot of mentions in this book! It's still a wonderful feat to win the Double but to do so then was extra special. Remember, it had only been done once before in the previous 71 years and I strongly believe it was more difficult to do then because teams were matched up much better than they are now.

We clinched the league that year at Tottenham in a very tough game but we still had to beat Liverpool in the FA Cup final at

Wembley. It was a boiling hot day and when they took the lead in extra-time I remember thinking, "Oh no, not again!", because I'd finished on the losing side in four previous Wembley finals. But Eddie Kelly scored a flukey equaliser before we won it thanks to Charlie George's great shot.

After the cup final I was absolutely shattered and I didn't have an ounce left to give – I was completely exhausted. I actually felt as flat as a pancake, but I had a couple of drinks to try and liven myself up. The next day we went to Islington Town Hall and there was a fantastic turn-out of about half a million people on the streets of Highbury. It was an unbelievable crowd. There was a photograph of me sitting on the steps of the Town Hall with my head in my hands and the caption in the newspaper was, "An emotional Frank McLintock", but actually I was suffering from a hangover!

Reading through this book has brought back many happy memories like that. It was nice, too, to see myself in the all-time Arsenal XI chosen by other ex-players a couple of years ago – it's a wonderful feeling when you get your fellow professionals putting your name forward and I was absolutely chuffed to be picked alongside the likes of Tony Adams, Liam Brady and Dennis Bergkamp.

Some of this book's more unusual contents were familiar to me – for example, that our goalkeeper Bob Wilson had the middle name 'Primrose' (although, as you can imagine, he tried to keep that under wraps), or that Muhammad Ali fought Henry Cooper at Highbury in 1966. I also knew that Arsenal played home games at – whisper it! – White Hart Lane during the Second World War, but I had no idea that London Zoo has named an anteater after Brazilian star Gilberto!

Now I have a box at Arsenal and I go there every week. I think Arsene Wenger has done a marvellous job over the years – as George Graham did before him. Arsene has a philosophy that football must be attractive to the eye and some of the teams he has had at the club have been absolutely breathtaking. I am sure his latest young team will soon be challenging for the championship and, hopefully, some of the current players will eventually stand comparison with the many great Arsenal legends who are featured in this cracking book.

Frank McLintock

Acknowledgements

The biggest shout out goes to Martin Cloake – who as a massive Spurs fan probably never expected to see his name in a book about Arsenal, but without whom I wouldn't have had the chance to write this book. Big thanks to my publisher Jim Drewett and my editor Clive Batty for all their work and guidance on this book, and I am very grateful to Bob Bond for his illustrations. Thanks go to Kieran Alger and Simon Hinde for giving me time away from my other work commitments to write this book, to Lindsay Melrose, Besim Sezer and Monil Narang for the Arsenal inspiration, to Shona Thind and Mark Stone for their help, to all my family and friends for their patience, to all the Gooners on Grandma Pearl's side of the family for showing me the red-and-white light in the first place, and finally to Rocky, Wrighty, Tone, Terence and the rest for making it a pleasure to follow the Arsenal.

Adam Gold

Author's note: All the stats in *The Arsenal Miscellany* are correct up until the start of the 2007/08 season.

— IN THE BEGINNING —

Arsenal's 27 million fans owe a huge debt of thanks to a young Scottish mechanical engineer, who packed his bags and bid farewell to Kirkcaldy while in his early 20s. David Danskin arrived at the Woolwich Armaments Factory in south-east London in 1886 and promptly set about forming a football team for the Scottish workers there.

Born in Fife in 1863, Danskin was the first in a long line of influential Scots at the club he founded (George Graham, Frank McLintock and Bruce Rioch were just a few of the others), and he went out and bought the initial football for the team that would one day become Arsenal FC. He rounded up Morris Bates, Jack Humble, Fred Beardsley – a former Nottingham Forest goalkeeper, who volunteered to ask his former club for some kit for the new side – and whoever he could find in the workshops who fancied a game.

Dial Square was an area in the centre of the workshops, named after the 1764 sundial placed over its entrance. And it was under this name that Danskin's team took to the field against the Eastern Wanderers on December 11th 1886. Playing on a swampy pitch that had no crossbars or markings, Dial Square won 6–0.

Two weeks later, on Christmas Day, the Dial Square FC players met at their local pub, the Royal Oak, to officially found their football club. As they were all workers at the Woolwich Arsenal, they decided on the name Royal Arsenal – partly because it sounded grand, but also as a nod to their choice boozer. This new team, Royal Arsenal, took to the field for the first time – in the dark red shirts donated by Nottingham Forest (see *Red is the Colour*, page 9) – on January 8th 1887 against Erith, who they thrashed 6–1 at home ground Plumstead Common.

David Danksin's achievement was formally commemorated 119 years later. At the spot where the old Woolwich Armament Factory stood, a plinth was installed in October 2005 to formally mark the origins of London's most successful club. As for Danskin, he lived to the age of 85, and enjoyed the world-beating feats of the Arsenal players in the 1930s and beyond.

— COME ON ARSENALS —

The English football club from north London is not the only one to go by the name of Arsenal. Four other sets of supporters around the world cheer on an Arsenal every week:

Berekum Arsenal
Ghana

This club had a Wimbledon-like rise to glory, gaining four promotions from 1995 to reach Ghana's Star Premier League. It's a glorious story for the team from a small town on the Ivory Coast border, formed out of respect to Arsenal FC, with Ian Wright their unofficial figurehead, the cannon their emblem, and the 'Gunners' their nickname.

Arsenal Kiev
Ukraine

Arsenal Kiev were formerly CSKA Kiev before they changed their name in 2002, after being bought by the Mayor of Kiev. The team that used to be a Soviet army side now play in the Ukraine Premier League, and have become regular contenders for a UEFA Cup or Champions League spot.

Arsenal de Sarandi
Argentina

This club from Buenos Aires plays in the Primera Division, having first reached the top flight in 2002. Formed in 1957, Arsenal de Sarandi were recently managed by Jorge Burruchaga, scorer of Argentina's winning goal in the 1986 World Cup final.

Arsenal Tula
Russia

The city of Tula, 300 miles south of Moscow, is known for a munitions factory similar to the one London's Arsenal were named after in Woolwich. During the Second World War the factory produced thousands of tanks, helping the Soviet army eventually defeat the Nazis. The team now plays in the Russian First Division. In 1996, Tula were among the first Russian sides to recruit Brazilian players and assisted by the samba skills of their latest crop of South Americans are currently challenging for a place in the Premier League.

In addition to these four clubs, top Portuguese side Braga, hailing from the northern Minho province, are nicknamed 'Arsenal do Minho'. Their association with the Gunners dates back to the 1930s when coach Jose Szabo returned from seeing Arsenal at Highbury and convinced the club to change their colours from green to red with white sleeves. Braga supporters dub themselves 'the Arsenalistas' and the club's youth team is even called Arsenal de Braga.

— MAKE MINE A DOUBLE —

Memories of the league and FA Cup Double in 1971:

"I would not normally say this as a family man, but I am going to ask you for the sake of this football club, to put your family second for the next month. You have the chance to put your names in the record books for all time."
Bertie Mee to the Arsenal players in the dressing room after they had beaten Stoke City in the FA Cup semi-final replay

"They talk about Bobby Moore and Dave Mackay as great captains, but for my money [Frank] McLintock is more inspiring than either of them."
Arsenal coach Don Howe

"Arsenal have got as much chance of being handed the title by Spurs as I have of being given the crown jewels. They are the last people we want winning the championship. Now we mean to round off our season by beating Arsenal."
Tottenham captain Alan Mullery before Arsenal's last league match of the season at White Hart Lane

"My first football memory was Charlie George's goal to win the Double in 1971. After that game I decided to become an Arsenal fan."
Paul Davis, Arsenal midfielder

"People say why did I lie on the floor after the goal, they said I was tired. But I think I was a lot cleverer than people thought."
Charlie George, describing a spot of time-wasting after hitting the winner in the FA Cup final

— FOREIGN BODIES —

Arsene Wenger demonstrated his skill at selecting talent from all around the planet when he became the first manager in English football history to select a 16–man squad of entirely foreign players. The team which thrashed Crystal Palace 5–1 in the Premiership on Valentine's Day, February 14th 2005, lined up as follows:

1. Jens Lehmann (Germany)
2. Lauren (Cameroon)
3. Gael Clichy (France)
4. Kolo Toure (Ivory Coast)
5. Pascal Cygan (France)
6. Robert Pires (France)
7. Patrick Vieira (France)
8. Edu (Brazil)
9. Jose Antonio Reyes (Spain)
10. Dennis Bergkamp (Holland)
11. Thierry Henry (France)

Subs: Manuel Almunia (Spain), Philippe Senderos (Switzerland), Cesc Fabregas (Spain), Robin van Persie (Holland), Mathieu Flamini (France)

— THE INVINCIBLES —

When the Gunners beat Manchester United 1–0 at Old Trafford in 2002, they became the first club since Preston in 1889 to go a whole season unbeaten away from home in the top division.

Two years later Arsenal went one better, by equalling the Lancashire club's incredible achievement of going an entire top-flight season without losing a single game. Comeback goals from Thierry Henry and Patrick Vieira gave the Gunners a 2–1 victory at home to Leicester City on May 15th 2004, sealing the record. Arsenal's achievement was all the more impressive as they had remained unbeaten in 38 games, compared to Preston's total of 22.

Here's how the top of the 2003/04 Premiership table looked at the end of the season:

	P	W	D	L	F	A	GD	Pt
Arsenal	**38**	**26**	**12**	**0**	**73**	**26**	**47**	**90**
Chelsea	38	24	7	7	67	30	37	79

— GUNNERS LEGENDS: ALEX JAMES —

Arsenal's greatest player of all time?

Arsenal's little Scottish playmaker of the 1930s has – despite all the talent of the Arsene Wenger era – a strong claim to being the club's greatest player of all time. Alex James arrived at Highbury from Preston in 1929 in an £8,750 transfer deal, a hefty sum in those days, and became a vital cog in manager Herbert Chapman's innovative 'M'-shaped attacking formation. Throughout his 264 appearances for the club, James was the creative force that helped make the Gunners into English football's first truly dominant club side.

Described by *The Times* as hitting passes "so stunningly beautiful that they could adorn the ceiling of the Sistine Chapel", James scored in Arsenal's first trophy success, the 1930 FA Cup victory over Huddersfield, and captained the club in the 1936 final. The inside-right – who had rheumatism and wore his trademark big baggy shorts to cover his long johns – sent through assist after assist for the likes of attackers Cliff Bastin and Ted Drake, helping Arsenal to four league title wins in five seasons. In the first of those championship successes in 1931, generous James set up many of his side's 127 goals – a record haul to this day. His control and passing skills were so perfect that his second manager at Arsenal, George Allison, once commented that, "no one like him had ever kicked a ball . . ."

A Scottish international, James began his career at Raith Rovers. In 1928 he played for Scotland in the 5–1 mauling of England by the legendary 'Wembley Wizards'. The most famous player of his day, fans across the country wanted to see James in action – and his celebrity was such that, while he was with Arsenal, he was given special perks denied other team members, such as permission to stay in bed until noon on match-days.

Like other players of his era, James was restricted by the Football League to earning no more than £8-per-week under the maximum wage ruling, making the annual £250 cheque he received from Selfridge's in Oxford Street for 'sports demonstration' a more than welcome bonus.

Name Alexander Wilson James
Born Mossend, Lanarkshire, September 14th 1901
Died June 1st 1953
Arsenal appearances 264
Arsenal goals 27
International appearances Scotland, 8

— FOOTBALL LEAGUE LEGENDS —

A staggering 18 Arsenal players made it into the Football League's list of '100 League Legends', created for its centenary celebrations in 1998. Here is the full list:

Player	Years played	Also played for
Alf Common	1900–15	Sunderland, Sheffield United, Middlesbrough, Preston
Charles Buchan	1910–29	Sunderland
Alex James	1925–38	Preston
Eddie Hapgood	1927–39	Shrewsbury Town
Cliff Bastin	1927–48	Exeter City
Wilf Copping	1929–39	Leeds United
David Jack	1919–34	Plymouth, Bolton
Ted Drake	1931–39	Southampton
Joe Mercer	1932–54	Everton
Tommy Lawton	1935–57	Burnley, Everton, Chelsea, Notts County, Brentford
Frank McLintock	1959–77	Leicester City, QPR
Pat Jennings	1962–85	Watford, Tottenham
Alan Ball	1962–84	Blackpool, Everton, Southampton, Bristol Rovers
Malcolm Macdonald	1968–79	Fulham, Luton, Newcastle United
Liam Brady	1973–90	West Ham
Tony Adams	1983–98*	
Dennis Bergkamp	1995–98*	

* Still playing at time of Football League centenary.

— SILVER SCREEN GUNNERS —

A team of Hollywood stars who have professed their love for north London's finest, or been spotted at Highbury or the Emirates:

Gillian Anderson
Kevin Costner
Colin Firth
Spike Lee
Sarah Michelle Gellar
Demi Moore
Nick Moran
David Schwimmer
David Soul
Joanne Whalley-Kilmer

— OCH AYE THE GUNNERS —

Arsenal began life as a football team for Scots in London. A young man called David Danskin created his team Dial Square – soon converted into Royal Arsenal FC – in 1886 after his move down from Kirkcaldy to work in the Woolwich Armaments Factory, south London (see *In the Beginning*, page 1).

And although the club went on to become one of the most successful in England, featuring players from every corner of the planet, there has remained intermittent Scottish involvement, in the form of characters from Alex James to George Graham. In all, 160 Scots to date have featured for the Gunners, including this team of internationals:

1. Bob Wilson
2. Ian Ure
3. Frank McLintock
4. Tommy Docherty
5. Alex James
6. Jimmy Logie
7. George Graham
8. David Herd
9. Charlie Nicholas
10. Tom Fitchie
11. Archie Macaulay

— RED IS THE COLOUR —

Strange though it sounds, Arsenal have to thank Nottingham Forest for playing in red.

When Dial Square were founded in 1886 three of their players – keeper Fred Beardsley and team mates Bill Parr and Charlie Bates – had previously turned out for Forest, and they persuaded their old club to donate a set of their dark red, 'redcurrant', kits for the new side. Twenty years later, in 1906, Arsenal performed a similar favour when they sold a set of kits to Sparta Prague, who have continued to wear a deep shade of red ever since.

A club crest first appeared on the Arsenal shirts in 1927 for the 1–0 FA Cup final defeat by Cardiff – after which Gunners keeper Dan Lewis complained that the new kit had been slippery, causing the ball to wriggle in for the winning goal.

The famous white sleeves made their debut not long afterwards in 1933 for a home match against Liverpool. Like many Arsenal innovations, the change was inspired by manager Herbert Chapman, who apparently got the idea for the new kit after spotting an Arsenal staff member in a red top with white sleeves. Apart from being a striking design, the switch helped the Gunners stand out against all the other teams who wore all red. Manager Billy Wright did revert the team strip back to all red for two seasons between 1965 and 1967, but soon after he was sacked the famous white sleeves were restored.

The gold kit the Gunners sported in the FA Cup final victory over Liverpool in 1950 eventually became the club's settled away colours – with variations of yellow and gold over the years. This included the much-loved 1989 League Championship-winning shirt of Michael Thomas and co – but also adidas's 'Squashed Banana' disaster of the early 1990s.

Meanwhile, other Arsenal kit misadventures over the years include blue-and-white-hooped socks, black-and-white-striped shirts, and the green-and-blue 'Bluebottle' away kit of the 1982/83 season.

The last big kit change came in the 2005/06 season, when the team turned out in the old-style redcurrant shade of red for the emotional last season at Highbury. Now installed at the Emirates Stadium, Arsenal FC are back in their distinctive red and white colours.

— GLOBAL GUNNERS —

Prior to the start of the 2007/08 season, no fewer than 84 foreign players from 35 different nations outside the British Isles had been on the books of Arsenal. Here's the full list:

Argentina: Fabian Caballero, Nelson Vivas
Australia: John Kosmina
Austria: Alex Manninger
Belarus: Alexander Hleb
Brazil: Julio Baptista, Denilson, Edu, Gilberto Silva, Juan, Paulinho, Silvinho
Cameroon: Lauren, Alexandre Song
Croatia: Eduardo da Silva, Davor Suker
Czech Republic: Michal Papadopulos, Tomas Rosicky
Democratic Republic of Congo: Carlin Itonga
Denmark: Nicklas Bendtner, John Jensen, Sebastian Svard
Estonia: Mart Poom
France: Jeremie Aliadiere, Nicolas Anelka, Gael Clichy, Pascal Cygan, Abou Diaby, Kaba Diawara, Mathieu Flamini, William Gallas, Remi Garde, Gilles Grimandi, David Grondin, Thierry Henry, Emmanuel Petit, Robert Pires, Armand Traore, Patrick Vieira, Guillaume Warmuz, Sylvain Wiltord
Germany: Jens Lehmann, Stefan Malz, Moritz Volz
Greece: Stathis Tavlaridis
Holland: Dennis Bergkamp, Giovanni van Bronckhorst, Glenn Helder, Gerry Keizer, Marc Overmars, Robin van Persie, Quincy Owusu-Abeyie
Iceland: Albert Gudmundsson, Siggi Jonsson, Olafur-Ingi Skulason
Italy: Arturo Lupoli
Ivory Coast: Emmanuel Eboue, Kolo Toure
Japan: Junichi Inamoto
Latvia: Igors Stepanovs
Liberia: Christopher Wreh
Libya: Jehad Muntasser
Lithunia: Tomas Danilevicius
Nigeria: Nwankwo Kanu
Norway: Pal Lydersen
Poland: Lukasz Fabianski
Portugal: Luis Boa Morte
South Africa: Daniel Le Roux

Spain: Manuel Almunia, Cesc Fabregas, Alberto Mendez, Jose Antonio Reyes
Sweden: Sebastian Larsson, Anders Limpar, Freddie Ljungberg, Stefan Schwarz, Rami Shabaan
Switzerland: Johan Djourou, Philippe Senderos
Togo: Emmanuel Adebayor
Ukraine: Oleg Luzhny
United States of America: Danny Karbassiyoon, Franki Simek
Yugoslavia: Vladimir Petrovic

— RED FACED —

While Highbury was being turned into an all-seater stadium in the early 1990s, its famous North Bank terrace had a mural erected in front of it to cover the reconstruction work. The 70-yard mural – the width of the pitch – featured the faces of happy home fans. Add noise from the rest of the stadium pumped out through a set of loud speakers and who would know the difference?

The era of the Mural End began badly, with a shock 4–2 reverse against Norwich City. But then things got very strange as people started to notice that all of the fans on the mural were white – something of an own goal, especially as Arsenal were proud of their record for having officially the most ethnically diverse fan base of any club in England. Happily, with a couple of pots of different coloured paint, the oversight was quickly put right.

— ARSENAL FEVER —

When Nick Hornby had his memoir *Fever Pitch* published in 1992, Arsenal fans finally found a read that summed up how they felt about the club (and to a certain extent, life). Arguably the most famous football book of all time, *Fever Pitch* drew on Hornby's own experience as a boy who discovers the joys of supporting Arsenal and remains an obsessive fan in adulthood.

The book has sold more than a million copies in the UK, and in 1997 was turned into a successful movie starring Colin Firth as Gunners-fixated schoolteacher Paul Ashworth. The plot focuses on Ashworth trying to juggle his lovelife with his love of Arsenal, as the Highbury side head towards the incredible title win of 1988/89.

— TWENTY YEARS A GUNNER —

The player who has appeared the most times in an Arsenal shirt is Irishman David O'Leary, who signed as an apprentice in 1973. When the 17-year-old centre-back took to the field for the 0–0 draw at Burnley on August 16th 1975, little did he know that he'd go on to play a massive further 721 matches for the Gunners.

Stoke Newington-born O'Leary – who moved to Dublin aged three – was a man who hit milestones in style. He overtook George Armstrong as Arsenal's record appearance maker against Norwich in 1989, scoring twice in a 4–3 win. Two decades after signing as an apprentice, he played his final match for the club in the 1993 FA Cup final victory over Sheffield Wednesday at Wembley.

Nicknamed 'Spider' because his numerous defensive interceptions and blocks almost gave the impression that he had more than the usual single pair of legs, O'Leary was the youngest Arsenal player to reach the 100 and 200 appearances mark. He also holds the record for most league games (558), and most FA Cup ties (70) and is one of a handful of players to have appeared in more than 1,000 matches at all levels. His durability was recognised when he had a Game Boy Color computer game named after him. More recently, he was the manager of Leeds United (1998–2002) and Aston Villa (2003–06).

The top ten Arsenal appearance makers are:

Player	Years played	Appearances
1. David O'Leary	1975–93	722
2. Tony Adams	1983–2002	669
3. George Armstrong	1962–77	621
4. Lee Dixon	1988–2002	619
5. Nigel Winterburn	1987–2000	584
6. David Seaman	1990–2003	564
7. Pat Rice	1967–80	528
8. Peter Storey	1965–76	501
9. John Radford	1963–76	481
10. Peter Simpson	1964–78	477

— MAGNIFIQUE —

Despite the ruthless efficiency of Ted Drake and Cliff Bastin under Herbert Chapman, and the exuberance and explosiveness of George Graham's star striker Ian Wright, one Arsenal goalscorer has topped the lot.

In the summer of 1999 a slim-looking French winger called Thierry Henry arrived at Highbury from Juventus. He didn't have a particularly outstanding goalscoring record but Arsene Wenger saw his potential and promptly turned him into a prolific striker. Within seven seasons, Henry had zoomed past Ian Wright's club record total of 185 goals, and rapidly overhauled Cliff Bastin's record of 150 league goals for the Gunners. Henry also holds the record for the most European goals for Arsenal with 50.

Before Arsenal's move to the Emirates stadium, he had a special relationship with Highbury, becoming the only Arsenal player ever to find the net there 100 times – a figure which included the last six Arsenal hat-tricks at the ground.

Henry heads a list of 16 players who have scored more than 100 goals for the Gunners:

Player	Total goals	Total games	100th-goal game	Strike rate
Thierry Henry	226	364	181st	62%
Ian Wright	185	288	143rd	64%
Cliff Bastin	178	396	174th	45%
John Radford	149	481	306th	31%
Jimmy Brain	139	232	144th	60%
Ted Drake	139	184	108th	76%
Doug Lishman	137	244	163rd	56%
Joe Hulme	125	374	307th	33%
David Jack	124	208	156th	60%
Dennis Bergkamp	120	401	296th	29%
Reg Lewis	118	176	152nd	67%
Alan Smith	115	347	251st	33%
Jack Lambert	109	161	149th	68%
Frank Stapleton	108	300	276th	36%
David Herd	107	180	165th	59%
Joe Baker	100	156	152nd	64%

Note: There should also be an honourable mention here for Paul Merson, who scored 99 Arsenal goals in 378 appearances.

—ASHBURTON GROVE —

The new Arsenal stadium at Ashburton Grove, named after sponsors Emirates, started life as a load of old rubbish. The site on which the magnificent ground now lies used to be a waste transfer station, which had to be moved to new premises nearby along with several other local businesses. The stadium now occupying the site dominates the area around, a symbol of the ambitions of the club under Arsene Wenger, and provides a daunting sight to visiting fans from the North and Midlands passing by in the trains arriving at nearby King's Cross.

It was way back in 1997, when the club came to the conclusion that Highbury could not be extended any further, that the search for a site for a bigger stadium had begun. King's Cross seemed ideal, keeping the club in the same part of north London, but construction would have been delayed until 2009 because of work on the new channel tunnel rail link – so Wembley, Alexandra Palace and Ashburton Grove were also considered.

It was a man called Anthony Spencer, a retail estate surveyor friend of then Gunners supremo David Dein, who noticed the 17-acre area at Ashburton Grove and realised its potential. "I got my *A to Z*, cut out Wembley Stadium and plonked it on to Ashburton Grove – it fitted," Spencer said. Eventually, plans to build a stadium at the council-owned site – a right turn out of Arsenal tube station rather than left for Highbury – appeared in November 1999, and construction began in January 2002.

Opened for the start of the 2006/07 season (not by the Queen as was planned because she had a bad back), the Emirates' 60,432 seats have more legroom than any other sporting arena in the country. The stadium's pitch is bigger than Highbury's traditionally small one – 113 x 76 metres, versus 105 x 70 metres – while 22,000 more fans watch each game played on the turf there than could fit into Highbury.

The first game at the world-class new £357m redevelopment was, fittingly, Dennis Bergkamp's testimonial against Ajax Amsterdam on July 22nd 2006, won 2–1 by the Gunners. The first competitive match was a 1–1 draw with Aston Villa on August 19th 2006, although in the 54th minute Villa's Olof Melberg took the honour of scoring the first competitive goal at the stadium, thus beginning an unfortunate trend for the opposition to score first at the new ground. For although Arsenal were only beaten once in that first season on their new home patch, they conceded the first goal in a staggering 13 out of the 27 Premiership, FA Cup, League Cup and Champions League matches played during 2006/07.

— PLAYERS OF THE YEAR —

Thierry Henry can add to his incredible array of Arsenal club honours that of being voted Player of the Year more times than anyone else. The Arsenal Football Supporters' Club picked 'Terence' on four occasions – more than any other player since the award was founded in 1967. Liam Brady and Tony Adams were both voted Player of the Year three times, while John Radford, Frank Stapleton and Ian Wright were each awarded the accolade twice.

Year	Player
1967	Frank McLintock
1968	John Radford
1969	Peter Simpson
1970	George Armstrong
1971	Bob Wilson
1972	Pat Rice
1973	John Radford
1974	Alan Ball
1975	Jimmy Rimmer
1976	Liam Brady
1977	Frank Stapleton
1978	Liam Brady
1979	Liam Brady
1980	Frank Stapleton
1981	Kenny Sansom
1982	John Hollins
1983	Tony Woodcock
1984	Charlie Nicholas
1985	Stewart Robson
1986	David Rocastle
1987	Tony Adams
1988	Michael Thomas
1989	Alan Smith
1990	Tony Adams
1991	Steve Bould
1992	Ian Wright
1993	Ian Wright
1994	Tony Adams
1995	David Seaman
1996	Martin Keown

1997	Dennis Bergkamp
1998	Ray Parlour
1999	Nigel Winterburn
2000	Thierry Henry
2001	Patrick Vieira
2002	Robert Pires
2003	Thierry Henry
2004	Thierry Henry
2005	Thierry Henry
2006	Jens Lehmann
2007	Cesc Fabregas

— GUNNER GUNNERS —

The Gunners lived up to their military moniker by sending 42 players to fight in the Second World War – more than any other football league club. Nine of those Arsenal footballers never returned after being killed in action.

One of the only two squad members who didn't join up was Cliff Bastin, who was barred from the military because he was almost deaf. Instead, he was stationed at Highbury, which was turned into an Air Raid Precautions Centre. While Bastin survived the war, the old stadium took some direct hits, with bombs landing on the North Bank and the Clock End. An Arsenal team of sorts continued to play during wartime, but their 'home' games – played at the home of arch rivals Spurs, White Hart Lane – did not count as official matches.

Arsenal's trainer Tom Whittaker, meanwhile, was based alongside Bastin at Highbury at the start of the war, until he joined the RAF and fought at D-Day. Whittaker was later given an MBE for his role as a squadron leader in the invasion of the French beaches. Two years after Arsenal finally returned to playing official matches at Highbury, Whittaker was made club manager, and went on to win two league championships and the FA Cup with his team.

— THEY SAID IT —

"We nearly didn't sign him because the letters did not fit on his shirt."
David Dein remembers the purchase of Giovanni Van Bronckhorst

"It sounds ridiculous, but I always put my watch into the right pocket of my trousers. If anybody wants to nick it, they'll know where to look now I suppose."
Steve Bould gives away his superstition

"I told my son Josh that Howard Wilkinson wanted Daddy to play for England. He told my daughter Olivia and they had tears in their eyes as they asked me, 'Does that mean you're not going to play for Arsenal any more?'"
Lee Dixon has some explaining to do to his kids

"I never thought of taking him off. It's nothing to worry about, it gives the face character."
George Graham discusses Andy Linighan's broken nose, after the big defender won the 1993 FA Cup for Arsenal

"Kenny Dalglish came on at the same time as me and everyone expected him to win it for Liverpool. But here I was, a ginger-haired nobody, setting up the winning goal for Arsenal."
Perry Groves shocks himself after the win over Liverpool in 1987's League Cup Final

"Ray is without doubt the funniest player I've ever trained with. It's so important to have players such as Ray involved with the group, for his contribution on the field and his spirit off it. I only wish I could understand more of what he says."
Gilles Grimandi enjoys the banter of the Romford Pele, Ray Parlour

"I started clapping myself, until I realised that I was Sunderland's manager."
Peter Reid agog at a Dennis Bergkamp goal against his side

"I think I lost my barnet flicking the ball on for all them years at the near post from Brian Marwood's corners."
Steve Bould thinks back to when he had hair

— MUSICAL GUNNERS —

A full squad of music biz people in tune with Arsenal:

Marc Almond (Soft Cell)
Graham Coxon (Blur)
Roger Daltry (The Who)
Ray Davies (The Kinks)
Dido
Tony Hadley (Spandau Ballet)
Aled Jones
Judge Jules
Gary Kemp (Spandau Ballet)
Martin Kemp (Spandau Ballet)
John Lydon, aka Johnny Rotten (The Sex Pistols)
Pete Tong
Sharleen Spiteri (Texas)

— COUNTRY CAPTAINS —

Eight English Arsenal players have experienced the honour of captaining their nation:

Player	Matches as England captain	Years
David Jack	4	1930–32
Eddie Hapgood	21	1934–39
George Male	6	1936–37
Alan Ball	6	1975
Tony Adams	15	1994–2000
David Platt	2	1996
David Seaman	1	1997
Martin Keown	1	2000

— GUNNERS LEGENDS: DENNIS BERGKAMP —

The non-flying Dutchman!

Then Arsenal manager Bruce Rioch made possibly the club's most important ever signing when he brought Dennis Berkgamp to Highbury from Inter Milan in 1995. The Dutchman didn't come cheap at £7.5 million, but over the years has more than justified his fee with some majestic strikes, not to mention all the goals he has laid on for team-mates. One of the most exciting players of his generation, the arrival of Bergkamp heralded the end of the 'Boring, Boring Arsenal' era of the previous decade.

Bergkamp stayed at Arsenal for 11 years, scoring 120 goals, dazzling English football in the process and paving the way for a whole generation of exciting foreign imports – from Gianfranco Zola to Eric Cantona.

Anyone who saw Bergkamp's wonder goals, such as those

against Leicester City in 1997 or Newcastle United in 2002, would probably agree that there's never been such a talent at bringing a speeding mid-air ball under control under pressure – and then burying it in the back of the net with a deft, immaculate finish.

Named after Denis Law (his parents added a second unnecessary 'n') and growing up idolising Glenn Hoddle, Bergkamp was actually a Tottenham fan. But Arsenal's north London rivals turned down the chance to take him to White Hart Lane after the Dutchman's unhappy two-year spell at Inter Milan, whom he had left from Ajax Amsterdam. Tottenham's loss was Arsenal's gain, with Bergkamp either scoring or setting up more than 40 per cent of Arsenal's goals over his first four seasons.

Along with the arrival of Arsene Wenger, Bergkamp's presence at Highbury transformed the whole club. Suddenly the club's dour footballing image, its reliance on the offside trap and efficient 1–0 victories was shattered. The new Arsenal was vibrant, exotic, brash and exciting and everyone wanted a part of it.

Revered by the Arsenal crowd and the English football community in general, Bergkamp flourished. He scored the best hat-trick BBC pundit Alan Hansen said he had ever seen against Leicester in August 1997, the finishes coming first, second and third in the BBC's Goal of the Month competition – the only time that ever happened. He was later voted PFA Players' Player of the Year and Football Writers' Association Footballer of the Year that season, and went on to come third in FIFA's World Player of the Year awards.

Throughout his Highbury career, Bergy formed key partnerships – primarily with fellow strikers Ian Wright, Nicolas Anelka and Thierry Henry, but also with midfielders like Robert Pires, Freddie Ljungberg and good friend Marc Overmars. He helped Arsenal to win two League and Cup Doubles in 1997/98 and 2001/02, the Premiership again in 2004 and two more FA Cups in 2003 and 2005.

In 1998 Arsene Wenger doubted there was a better player in the world: "If there is then I have not seen him," the gaffer pondered.

Apart from the odd snappy tackle which earned him the occasional booking, Bergkamp's only flaw was a deep fear of air travel, stemming from an incident at the 1994 World Cup when a journalist joked that a bomb was on the plane the Dutch squad were about to board. As a result, he often didn't play for Arsenal in European away games because the distances involved ruled out travelling by train or car. Inevitably, he was subsequently dubbed 'The Non-Flying Dutchman', a nickname that became even more appropriate when his phobia led him to quit international football in 2000.

Fittingly Bergkamp's testimonial was the first match to be played at Arsenal's new Emirates Stadium, the Gunners beating Ajax 2–1 as an emotional 54,000 fans came to spend just one more Saturday afternoon 'walking in a Bergkamp wonderland'.

Name Dennis Nicolaas Maria Bergkamp
Nickname Beavis, Bergy, The Iceman
Born Amsterdam, The Netherlands, May 10th 1969
Arsenal appearances 345
Arsenal goals 120
International appearances Holland, 79
International goals 36

— ON THE SAME WAVELENGTH —

Perhaps as a precursor to their almost telepathic understanding as a strike partnership on the pitch, Dennis Bergkamp and Ian Wright linked up almost as soon as the Dutchman had set foot on English soil. For when Bergkamp was driving to Arsenal to have his medical in the summer of 1995, the pair bumped into each other in a petrol station on the M25.

Bergkamp had just arrived from the Netherlands, and thought he was about to have his first introduction to London road rage with the driver of a car in front of him at a garage where he had stopped for petrol, when he realised the over-excited individual making gestures at him was none other than Ian Wright. Arsenal's star striker had just heard on the radio that Bergkamp had joined the Gunners, and when he realised it was Bergkamp in the car behind him, rushed up to give his new Dutch team-mate a big Wrighty hug.

"It really was the biggest coincidence I've ever known," said Bergkamp later. "It was amazing that I met the person who was going to be my playing partner for the next few years like that."

— MOVING UP NORTH —

Arsenal began life in 1886 as Dial Square, a football team based at the Woolwich Arsenal armaments factory in south London. But after nearly 40 years south of the river, Arsenal became a north London side with the move to new stadium Highbury, just before the First World War.

The man behind the Gunners move to Highbury in 1913 was Arsenal chairman Henry Norris, a former director of Fulham FC. A slight man with a huge moustache and a ruthless charm, Norris was ambitious and dynamic. As football grew in popularity, he saw the potential of having a truly great London team to rival the dominance of the well-established northern and midlands clubs.

A property developer and later a politician, Norris had many strings he could pull in the city, and first attempted to merge Fulham and Woolwich Arsenal into one big club. When this idea was rejected by the Football League, Norris decided he would move Woolwich Arsenal to a new site, ideally one with good transport links and some distance from the main catchment area of any other club. He looked at Battersea and Harringay as options, before finally settling on the sports grounds of St John's College of Divinity in Highbury, handily situated next to Gillespie Road tube station. Norris coughed up £20,000, the Archbishop of Canterbury handed over a 21-year lease (eventually selling the site outright in 1925) and Arsenal had their new stadium in Highbury.

This development was extremely bad news for Tottenham Hotspur. They had pretty much had north London's football market to themselves, competing only with Clapton Orient. Now there was another large club on their doorstep, and despite Tottenham's appeals, Arsenal were reborn as a north London outfit. 'Woolwich' was swiftly dropped from the name, and the club was known informally as 'The Arsenal' for the start of the 1913/14 season.

— BADGE OF HONOUR —

The famous AFC cannon is one of the most recognised logos in world football, celebrating the club's roots having been formed by workers at the armaments factory in Woolwich, south London.

While Arsenal have always had a cannon insignia, the design around it has changed many times since the club's founding in the 19th century. Initially, the symbol incorporated Woolwich's coat of arms, featuring three cannons pointing vertically into the air like chimneys, but that was replaced in 1922, when a thunderous-looking cannon pointing east took over, next to the words 'The Gunners'. In 1925 this cannon was redesigned and pointed west – some fans claim because Spurs, to the east, weren't much of a threat at that stage – until 1949 when a large letter A was inserted onto the badge.

At the same time, Arsenal's championship win a year earlier in 1948 was commemorated with a motto, *Victoria Concordia Crescit*. The phrase roughly translates from Latin as 'Victory Through Harmony', and was suggested by match-day programme editor Harry 'Marksman' Homer who felt that the title triumph was the result of the close-knit nature of the Arsenal squad. The motto was reproduced in gothic text, giving the Arsenal logo a sense of history and class. It was at this time, too, that many clubs started wearing crests on their shirts for every game, rather than just for an important match such as the FA Cup final.

That famous crest stayed in place for the next half a century, with only minor tweaks, although only a single cannon actually appeared on the shirts in the 60s, 70s and early 80s. Then, in 2002, the club decided to revamp the badge, partly because of copyright problems surrounding the old crest. The result was an updated red, white and blue crest with a clean-outline cannon (facing east again – was this down to worries about Tottenham eventually mounting a challenge in north London again?) and the word 'Arsenal' appearing in a very modern-looking typeface. Initially, many fans disliked the new branding, but the majority soon warmed to their team's new-look insignia, especially as it seemed to reflect Arsene Wenger's look-forward not back ambitions.

— SLUG 'IM, 'ENRY! —

Legendary British heavyweight boxer Sir Henry Cooper filled Highbury to the rafters when he fought with world champ Muhammad Ali. The stadium was crammed with 45,973 fight fans as the American heavyweight champion of the world took on London's finest on May 21st 1966.

Cooper was an Arsenal supporter who used to come to matches, and also used the same physio as the Gunners. The atmosphere was intense as Londoners shouted Cooper's name. He walked out into the ring that had been erected by Charlie George and some of the other Arsenal youngsters and staffers, his mind focused on beating 'The Greatest', the man he had knocked down in their first fight at Wembley three years earlier when Ali was still known as Cassius Clay.

The fight got underway, with Hollywood stars such as Lee Marvin in attendance. They fought six rounds, until Ali cut Cooper above the eye, leading referee Tommy Little to stop the bout and declare Ali the winner. The East Ender with the punch nicknamed 'Enry's 'Ammer had been defeated, but he will always be remembered as a true Highbury sporting hero.

— GILBERTO THE ANTEATER —

Arsenal's Gilberto Silva has an anteater named after him at London Zoo. While the creature was born in London, it is descended from anteaters in Brazil, and was called Gilberto by Arsenal fan Peter Findlay, who won the chance to give him a name. Gilberto the footballer went to meet his namesake at the zoo, and told staff he hoped the two would be like brothers. While Gilberto the anteater is likely to reach two feet in height, four feet in length and weigh eight stone, his human counterpart is already fully grown at 6ft 3in, and weighs in at a little under 13 stone.

— WHAT'S IN A NAME? —

Arsenal have been known as 'The Arsenal' at times since moving to Highbury in 1913, but have had four official names since their foundation in 1886. These are:

1886	Dial Square
1887–91	Royal Arsenal
1891–1913	Woolwich Arsenal
1913–	Arsenal

— THE DRUGS DON'T WORK —

In January 1925 Arsenal manager Leslie Knighton tried to give his struggling side an edge for a vital FA Cup tie against West Ham by handing out pills containing a mixture of unknown substances.

The unlikely episode began while Knighton was preparing for the contest, when he was visited by a Gunners-supporting Harley Street doctor. After hearing of the team's difficulties, the medic offered Knighton some 'courage pills' to give his players. Waving away the manager's questions, the doctor refused to say what was in the tablets, but stressed that they were legal in sport and would be just the pick-me-up the underperforming Gunners needed.

Somewhat amazingly, Knighton took his advice and gave each of his men a pill before the match. However, foggy conditions led to the game being called off. Back in the changing room, meanwhile, the players were experiencing the side effects of the drug, becoming very hyped up and terribly thirsty. Knighton was not put off, though, and handed out the pills again at the rearranged fixture – bizarrely, this was also postponed.

At the third attempt, the tablet-taking Gunners were all over the Hammers but couldn't find a way through, the game ending 0–0. Before the replay, the players refused to take the pills, complaining the previous doses had caused insatiable thirst and other strange side effects. Knighton was forced to relent, and his drug-free team still couldn't beat West Ham – the game ending in a 2–2 draw. The second replay was decided by a single Hammers goal, Arsenal going down 1–0.

The Harley Street pills were never handed round at Arsenal again and Knighton was soon replaced as manager by Herbert Chapman.

— GUNNER BROTHERS —

Denis and Leslie Compton are the most famous brothers to play for Arsenal, helping to bring the FA Cup home to Highbury in 1950. The incredible sporting Compton duo also played for Middlesex at cricket, winning the County Championship in the same year as their cup triumph.

The Comptons represented England at both football and cricket, centre-half Leslie winning his first cap at the age of 38 to become his country's oldest debutant. Denis, meanwhile, is still remembered as one of the finest middle order batsmen English cricket has produced. He also played on the wing for England in a number of unofficial wartime football matches.

More recently, Justin Hoyte has been followed into the Arsenal set-up by younger brother Gavin. Although not officially an Arsenal player, Kolo's brother Yaya Toure had a trial under Arsene Wenger in 2003. The two Ivory Coast internationals appeared alongside each other in some pre-season friendly games, including a 0–0 draw with Barnet. Yaya, though, was not signed up by 'Le Professeur' in the end, and returned to Belgian club Beveren.

George Buist and Robert Buist
Joe Bradshaw and William Bradshaw
Andrew Neave and David Neave
Thomas Rippon and Willis Rippon
Charles Satherwaite and Joe Satherwaite
Denis Compton and Leslie Compton
Danny Clapton and Denis Clapton
Stefan Gislason and Valur Gislason
Michael Black and Tommy Black
Gavin Hoyte and Justin Hoyte

— IAN WRITE, WRITE, WRITE —

'We're by far the most intelligent team, the world has ever seen!' Arsenal fans from the literary world:

Melvyn Bragg
David Frost
Nick Hornby, author of *Fever Pitch*
Michael Moore, author of *Stupid White Men*
Piers Morgan, former editor of *The Mirror*
Andrew Motion (Poet Laureate, 1999–)

— GUNNERS LEGENDS: CLIFF BASTIN —

A footballer every defence feared

Cliff 'The Boy' Bastin is one of English football's all-time greats. In the pulsating Arsenal side of the 1930s, Bastin was one of the few players to win the lot – five League Championships and two FA Cups. For his skill on the ball, vision and deadly finishing, Bastin was renowned in European football. He scored 178 goals for Arsenal – a figure that would not be bettered until Ian Wright and later Thierry Henry arrived more than half a century later – despite playing on the wing rather than the centre of attack.

Bastin was signed by Arsenal thanks to Gunners' boss Herbert Chapman's sharp eye for a good player. In 1929 Chapman went to watch a player at Watford, but it was a 17-year-old left-winger for the Hornets' opponents, Exeter City, who really impressed him.

Young Bastin had hit six goals in 17 games for his home town club, including two on his home debut, and was happy there – but a move to Arsenal was impossible to resist.

The lad from Devon was put straight into the first team at Highbury, and he blossomed in Chapman's 'WM' formation. In 1930 he became one of the youngest players to appear in the FA Cup final, aged just 18 and 43 days when he featured against Huddersfield at Wembley. Always a threat to the opposition, he shared 53 goals with right-winger Joe Hulme during the 1932/33 title-winning season.

With his speed and accuracy, Bastin was a footballer every defence feared. He had a strong mentality too, which meant he was an ideal penalty taker and often came up with the goods in the big, high-pressure matches. Hugo Meisel – the Austrian credited with creating the World Cup competition – claimed that Austria would have won the 1934 World Cup if Arsenal's Cliff Bastin had been playing for them.

As it was, Bastin played 21 games for England, scoring 12 goals, and was one of the seven Arsenal players who featured in the violent 'Battle of Highbury' England match against the Italian world champions in 1934 (see *The Battle of Highbury*, page 35). Bizarrely, during the Second World War, the Italians boasted that they had captured Bastin in Crete in a propaganda coup. In fact, the winger's near deafness made him unfit for military service and he spent the entire conflict at Highbury, assisting in air-raid-warning duty.

Bastin was only 27 and in his prime when the war interrupted his playing career. He played on briefly after the end of hostilities, but was hampered by a leg injury. In 1947 he retired to write an autobiography and run a pub in his beloved Devon, where Exeter City eventually named a terrace at St James Park the Cliff Bastin Stand.

Name Clifford Sydney Bastin
Nickname 'Boy' Bastin
Born Heavitree, Devon, March 14th 1912
Died December 4th 1991
Arsenal appearances 392
Arsenal goals 178
International appearances England, 21
International goals 12

— MANAGING EXPECTATIONS —

Including caretakers, Arsenal have had 23 different managers. The most successful were Herbert Chapman, who led the club to its first trophy, the FA Cup in 1930, and two league titles before his premature death in January 1934; his successors, George Allison and Tom Whittaker, who both won three trophies; Bertie Mee, who secured the club's first European triumph and domestic Double; George Graham, who led the Gunners to six triumphs in the 1980s and 1990s before his Highbury career ended in disgrace; and, finally, Arsene Wenger, the most successful manager in the club's history with three league titles and four FA Cup victories to his name.

Here's the full list of Gunners bosses:

Reign	Manager	Honours
Aug 1894–July 1897	Sam Hollis	
Aug 1897–March 1898	Thomas Mitchell	
March 1898–May 1899	George Elcoat	
Aug 1899–May 1904	Harry Bradshaw	
July 1904–Feb 1908	Phil Kelso	
Feb 1908–May 1915	George Morrell	
May 1919–June 1925	Leslie Knighton	
June 1925–Jan 1934	Herbert Chapman	League (1930/31, 1932/33), FA Cup (1930)
Jan 1934–June 1934	Joe Shaw (caretaker)	League (1933/34)
June 1934–May 1947	George Allison	League (1934/35, 1937/38), FA Cup (1936)
June 1947–Oct 1956	Tom Whittaker	League (1947/48, 1952/53), FA Cup (1950)
Oct 1956–May 1958	Jack Crayston	
July 1958–May 1962	George Swindin	
May 1962–June 1966	Billy Wright	
June 1966–May 1976	Bertie Mee	League and FA Cup Double (1970/71), European Fairs Cup (1970)

July 1976–Dec 1983	Terry Neill	FA Cup (1979)
Dec 1983–March 1986	Don Howe	
March 1986–May 1986	Steve Burtenshaw (caretaker)	
June 1986–Feb 1995	George Graham	League (1988/89, 1991/92), FA Cup and League Cup Double (1993), League Cup (1987), European Cup Winners' Cup (1994)
Feb 1995–May 1995	Stewart Houston (caretaker)	
June 1995–Aug 1996	Bruce Rioch	
Aug 1996	Stewart Houston (caretaker)	
Sep 1996	Pat Rice (caretaker)	
Sep 1996 –	Arsene Wenger	League and FA Cup Double (1997/98, 2001/02), League (2003/04), FA Cup (2002, 2005)

— GHOSTING IN AT THE FAR POST—

Highbury is said to have been haunted by a dead horse. The animal died on the ground in the 1930s when Highbury's new art deco stands were under construction. The fatal incident happened after a contractor's horse and cart fell into a huge hole beneath the North Bank. A rescue bid proved fruitless, so the horse was put down and its remains covered up.

Years later, Arsenal supporters claimed to hear anguished equine cries from the North Bank – but when the stand was redeveloped again in the 1990s, mysteriously, no horse bones were found.

— WALKING BILLBOARDS —

The Japanese electronics firm JVC were Arsenal's first ever sponsors, their logo going on to adorn the club's shirts for 18 years from 1981 to 1999.

When this arrangement finally came to a close, the computer games company SEGA took over, with their brand name appearing on the away kits and the name of their console Dreamcast on the home shirts. That deal ran from the 1999/2000 season through to the end of the Double triumph in 2001/02.

The next outfit to associate themselves chest-high with the Gunners were mobile phone firm 02. The kits worn from 2002/03 carried their insignia until Arsenal left Highbury and the 02 deal behind at the end of the 2005/06 season.

Part of the transaction that created the Emirates stadium was that the airline could have their logo on Arsenal shirts for eight years from the start of the 2006/07 campaign. The high flyers spent a jumbo £100m for the sponsorship rights, and now the logo 'Fly Emirates' is a feature on the famous red-and-white jerseys.

— THE TRIPLE DOUBLE —

If there's one way to engrave your name in English footballing history, it's by winning the mythical Double. For a team to get their hands on both the League Championship and FA Cup trophies in the same season proves total dominance in the country, and no club has managed this more times than Arsenal.

The Gunners have won the Double on three occasions to date: in 1970/71, when Charlie George's extra-time winner in the FA Cup final brought glory to the club; in 1997/98, Nicholas Anelka inspiring Arsene Wenger's side to victory at Wembley; and in 2001/02, when legendary skipper Tony Adams lifted both trophies before hanging up his boots.

Arsenal's fierce rivals in the 1990s and 2000s, Manchester United, are the only other team to register three Doubles, all within five years of each other in 1994, 1996 and 1999. The other clubs to win the Double are Preston (1888/89), Aston Villa (1896/97), Tottenham (1960/61) and Liverpool (1985/86).

— MURDER MOST FOUL —

Confusion reigned in Spain in 1952, when a newspaper there reported that a suspicious death had occurred on the pitch during an Arsenal match at Highbury.

The headline translated as: 'ARSENAL PLAYER MURDERED DURING A MATCH. SCOTLAND YARD INVESTIGATES!'

The report continued: "An English footballer of the Arsenal has been killed during a football match played at Highbury. Scotland Yard has opened an inquiry. The players who took part in the match have been questioned, as well as the referee, who would appear to be the murderer."

Shockwaves rippled through the Spanish football-following public. Luckily, however, the paper had mistaken French newspaper *L'Equipe*'s serialisation of fictional work *The Arsenal Stadium Mystery* for reality, and run the story as true.

— HIT SQUADS —

The Arsenal team have hit the charts a few times with songs recorded to help gee them on to victory. Most famous was 'Good Old Arsenal' sung to the tune of 'Rule Britannia', with lyrics written by none other than supersize-chinned football pundit Jimmy Hill. It reached 16 in the charts. Here is the full list of records released by the Arsenal team:

Single	Year
'Here We Go Again'	1932
'Good Old Arsenal'	1971
'Arsenal, We're On Your Side'	1972
'Roll Out The Red Carpet'	1978
'Super Arsenal'	1979
'We're Back Where We Belong'	1989
'Shouting For The Gunners'	1993
'Hot Stuff'	1998
'Arsenal Number One'	2000

— GUNNERS LEGENDS: IAN WRIGHT —

Ian Wright, Wright, Wright!

"Ian Wright, Wright, Wright. So good they named him thrice." So said BBC commentator Jonathan Pearce about the onetime Woolwich plasterer who became Arsenal's greatest-ever goalscorer.

Signed by George Graham in 1991 for a club record £2.5m fee from Crystal Palace, the man who'd been playing Sunday league football until just before his 22nd birthday was set to install himself as one of Arsenal's most popular ever players.

Wright won the Golden Boot in his first season at Highbury, banging in 29 goals, including many of his trademark chips from the edge of the box into the top corner. For five seasons he was every goalkeeper's nightmare, collecting the ball with his back to goal, turning and firing in looping drives from every angle and picking up FA Cup, League Cup and Cup Winners' Cup medals along the way. With his goals, along with his accompanying beaming smile and exuberant personality, Wrighty is remembered for carrying the team's attack almost single-handedly as Arsenal waned in the mid-1990s.

Wright was Arsenal's Player of the Year in 1992 and 1993, and smashed in goal after goal, leaping into the air in ecstasy after each one. The striker's obvious passion for the club made him a fans' favourite.

Towards the end of his Highbury career, Wrighty's finishing skills and enthusiastic approach were rewarded with more titles and records. He finally won the League title he'd always dreamt about in 1998, and in the same season beat Cliff Bastin's 59-year-old record of 178 Arsenal goals. After his second, record-breaking strike against Bolton on September 13th 1997, Wright revealed a vest under his shirt that read: *179 – Just Done It.* "To be mentioned in the same breath as Ted Drake and Cliff Bastin is a great honour," he said, reflecting on his achievement.

"My image of the day will always be of the joy of the whole team when he broke his record," said Arsene Wenger in a post-match tribute to Wrighty. "That shows how he is accepted by everyone. It was an historic moment. Maybe it will be 100 years before the record goes again. After all, it has stood for so long and Arsenal had some great strikers." For once, Wenger was wrong. The rise and rise of Thierry Henry meant that the Frenchman assumed the greatest-ever goalscorer crown from Wrighty in 2005.

The effervescent Wright ended his Arsenal days in the summer of 1998 for short spells at West Ham United and Celtic, among others, before becoming a regular TV and radio presenter and pundit. The Wright name lives on in today's football. His adopted son, Shaun Wright-Phillips, plays for Chelsea and England; Shaun's half-brother, Bradley, is at Southampton; and his own son, Brett, is on the books of Reading.

Name Ian Edward Wright MBE
Nickname Wrighty, Satchmo
Born Woolwich, London, November 3rd 1963
Arsenal appearances 288
Arsenal goals 185
International appearances England, 33
International goals 9

— THE OVERALL PICTURE —

Arsenal lie second in the overall table for Premiership results since the new league was formed in 1992. Out of the 15 Premiership seasons to date, Arsenal have finished first or second eight times. Incidentally, Chelsea are third, Liverpool fourth and Spurs down in seventh place. This is how the top two compare:

Pos.Team	Seasons	P	W	D	L	F	A	GD	Pts	Titles	2nd	Pts av.
1. Man Utd	15	582	367	131	84	1140	516	624	1232	9	3	82.1
2. Arsenal	15	582	308	157	117	974	516	458	1081	3	5	72.1

— THE BATTLE OF HIGHBURY —

Five months after Italy won the second-ever World Cup in 1934, England – who had not bothered to enter the tournament – set out to prove they were the real champions in a match between the two countries at Highbury.

The England team included seven Arsenal players, a record number from just one club: keeper Frank Moss, full-backs George Male and Eddie Hapgood, hard-man Wilf Copping, winger Cliff Bastin and forwards Ray Bowden and Ted Drake.

Supposedly a friendly, the match turned into a violent affair bordering on all-out warfare that would later be dubbed 'the Battle of Highbury'. After a Ted Drake tackle broke Luisito Monti's foot and the Italian player was forced to leave the field, the visitors went beserk and spent the rest of the half determined to seek revenge.

With the Italians more concerned with kicking their opponents, England missed a penalty and then swept into a 3–0 lead in 15 minutes, including one from Drake when England were down to 10 men with captain Hapgood off the pitch being treated for an elbow in the face.

In the second half the Italians finally started playing football and staged a second-half fightback, with Giuseppe Meazza, a striker who later gave his name to the Milan stadium, hitting the bar and scoring twice. But in the pouring rain England grimly held on, with Arsenal keeper Frank Moss denying the world champions an equaliser.

At the end of the match England were a team of walking wounded. Hapgood's nose was broken, Brown's arm was broken, John Barker's hand was strapped and the entire team was battered and bruised. Nevertheless, November 14th 1934 went down in Highbury history as the day 'Arsenal' beat the world champions.

— BEST GUNNERS NICKNAME XI —

1. Bob 'Willow' Wilson
2. Oleg 'Horse' Luzhny
3. Wilf 'Iron Man' Copping
4. Nigel 'Nutty' Winterburn
5. Liam 'Chippy' Brady
6. George 'Stroller' Graham
7. Julio 'The Beast' Baptista
8. Anders 'Super Swede' Limpar
9. Malcolm 'Supermac' Macdonald
10. Alan 'Smudger' Smith
11. Ray 'Romford Pele' Parlour

— BOXERS V JOCKEYS —

Highbury played host to ten rather unusual football matches between 1951 and 1960. The first eight of these involved a team of boxers taking on a team of jockeys, to raise money for the Sportsman's Aid Society. The tenth and final contest saw a combined team of boxers and jockeys play a celebrity XI that included soon-to-be James Bond actor Sean Connery. Among the boxers to appear in some of these games was British heavyweight champion Henry Cooper.

The renowned boxing referee Sam Russell first came up with idea of the fixture, and usually managed to get Arsenal players such as Jimmy Logie, Arthur Shaw or one of the Compton brothers to referee the matches, with a racing personality running one line and a boxing official the other. The annual event always drew big crowds to the stadium, with one side wearing the Arsenal kit and the other sporting Spurs shirts. The first such match on April 2nd 1951 was notable for being the first game to be played under floodlights at Highbury.

— GUNNERS LEGENDS: FRANK MCLINTOCK —

Frank McLintock: 1971 Double skipper

Influential Scottish defender Frank McLintock was the first man to lift the Double for Arsenal. Described by coach Don Howe as 'the perfect captain', McLintock also skippered the Gunners in three other Wembley cup finals and was the first Arsenal captain to get his hands on a European trophy, the 1970 Fairs Cup.

The success he enjoyed at Highbury was all the sweeter for the rugged central defender, as the early part of his career was marked by disappointment. With his previous club, Leicester City, McLintock was on the losing side in two FA Cup finals, in 1961 and 1963, although he did pick up a winners' medal in the League Cup in 1964. In the same year he signed for Arsenal for a British record fee of £80,000, but it wasn't until the end of the decade that McLintock's Gunners really started firing.

After a shock League Cup final defeat by Third Division Swindon in 1969, the Scot enjoyed his first triumph with the north Londoners the following year. 3–1 down after the first leg of the Inter-City Fairs Cup final against Belgian side Anderlecht, McLintock led his side to a 3–0 triumph in the return at Highbury and was mobbed by joyful Gooners in a pitch invasion at the end. But if the Arsenal supporters enjoyed that victory, then the manner of the Double win the following season was beyond all expectations.

McLintock was inspirational at centre-back at the heart of a defence which conceded just 29 goals in 42 league games. By a quirk of fate, Arsenal had to avoid defeat against Tottenham at White Hart Lane in their final league match to win the title. Ray Kennedy's header and Bob Wilson's heroics in goal brought victory to the Gunners, clinching the championship ahead of runners-up Leeds. Five days later, in the FA Cup final against Liverpool, Arsenal went a goal down in extra time. Typically, it was McLintock who roused his struggling side to score two goals back and secure the cup and the Double. In the same season, Frank's leadership qualities were acknowledged when he was voted Footballer of the Year.

As a tough-nut 'Mr Arsenal' who led by example, McLintock was the template for Tony Adams in years to come. Reluctantly, he left Highbury in 1973 to see out his playing days with QPR. Following his retirement, he had stints in management at Leicester and Brentford before becoming a successful media pundit.

Name Frank McLintock (MBE)
Born Glasgow, December 28th 1939
Arsenal appearances 401
Arsenal goals 32
International appearances Scotland, 9

— ISLINGTON'S FINEST —

Highbury and the Emirates Stadium's borough of Islington has produced several boys that went on to play for the club in the back yard. Here they are:

Dave Bacuzzi
Jay Bothroyd
Mark Flatts
Charlie George
John Halls
Eddie McGoldrick
Ryan Smith
Paolo Vernazza
Chris Whyte
Raphael Meade

— THE LEGENDS PICK THE ARSENAL TEAM —

In the early 2000s, 52 of the greatest players from the club's history voted for their best ever Arsenal XI. The players, lined up below in team formation, to poll the most votes were:

Pat Jennings (28)

Lee Dixon (19)   Kenny Sansom (29)
      Tony Adams (43)   Frank McLintock (25)

George Armstrong (29)   Robert Pires (24)
      Liam Brady (42)   Patrick Vieira (45)

    Thierry Henry (42)   Ian Wright (22)

Subs:
David Seaman (11), Bob McNab (12), Pat Rice (13), David O'Leary (13) Dennis Bergkamp (13)

— OLD TRAFFORD WARS —

The rivalry between Arsenal and Manchester United is one of the fiercest in English football. Occasionally, the antipathy between the two sides has erupted into outright violence, as in these three infamous incidents:

- On October 20th 1990 a minor confrontation between Manchester United defender Dennis Irwin and Arsenal midfielder Anders Limpar during the clubs' encounter at Old Trafford sparked a 21-man brawl – Gunners goalkeeper David Seaman was the only player who didn't get involved in the unseemly scenes. Arsenal, who incidentally won the match 1–0, were later deducted two points as a punishment but still went on to win the championship. Meanwhile, United were deemed to be less culpable for the incident and were deducted just a single point.

- A typically feisty meeting between the two sides at Old Trafford during the 2003/04 season got even hotter when Arsenal skipper Patrick Vieira was sent off for a foul on United striker Ruud van Nistelrooy ten minutes from time. The Arsenal players were outraged, believing that the Dutch international had over-reacted in an attempt to get Vieira shown a second yellow card. Nursing this grievance a number of Arsenal players couldn't help gloating when, in injury time, Nistelrooy smashed a penalty against the bar. When the final whistle blew on a tempestuous 0–0 draw, Gunners defenders Martin Keown and Lauren violently jostled van Nistelrooy as the players trooped towards the tunnel. Arsenal were subsequently fined a record £175,000 for failing to control their players, and four members of the Gunners team were also banned for a total of nine matches.

- The following season, Arsenal's 49-match unbeaten run in the Premiership came to an end with a 2–0 defeat at Old Trafford. Another spiky on-field encounter descended into near anarchy in the tunnel after the match as the two sides scuffled and United manager Alex Ferguson was allegedly pelted with soup and lumps of pizza. Arsene Wenger played down the incident but landed in hot water himself when he turned on Gunners hate figure van Nistelrooy, labelling the striker "a cheat" – a comment which earned the Arsenal boss a hefty £15,000 fine.

— BEFORE THEIR TIME —

A list of Gunners who sadly passed away prematurely:

Player	Age	Year	Cause of death
George Armstrong	55	2000	Brain haemorrhage: Died on Arsenal's training ground.
Bob Benson	33	1916	Overexertion: Called upon to play for Arsenal during WWI while not match fit. Died in the changing room.
Alexander Caie	36	1914	No details available.
Tommy Caton	30	1993	Heart attack: Apparently stressed about ankle injury about to cause possible retirement.
Herbert Chapman	56	1934	Pneumonia: Contracted after watching an Arsenal third-team game while unwell with a heavy cold.
Andy Ducat	56	1941	Heart attack: While batting for Surrey at Lord's in a WWII-time cricket match.
Niccolo Galli	17	1999	Road traffic accident.
Alex James	51	1953	Cancer.
Jack Lambert	38	1940	Road traffic accident.
Joseph Powell	26	1896	Blood poisoning: After breaking his arm in a match for Arsenal.
Sidney Pugh	24	1944	RAF plane crash during WWII.
David Rocastle	33	2001	Cancer.
Tom Whittaker	58	1956	Heart attack: Over-worked with stress of being Arsenal's secretary-manager.

— GUNNERS LEGENDS: HERBERT CHAPMAN —

Herbert Chapman: Football visionary

Arsenal as we know it would quite simply not exist if it hadn't been for Herbert Chapman. Such was his impact, not just on the Gunners, but on the entire way football was viewed as a spectator sport, that he will be remembered as one of the game's all-time great managers and thinkers.

Chapman joined Arsenal as manager in 1925, having won three league titles in a row with Huddersfield Town. "I am going to make this the greatest club in the world," he said, shortly after arriving at Highbury.

He quickly set about turning the club from top-flight newcomers to the most famous team in England, encouraging star striker Charlie Buchan, finding unknown talents in keeper Frank Moss and winger Cliff Bastin, and signing class acts Alex James and David Jack (Chapman successfully getting the Bolton Wanderers negotiators drunk during the Jack deal).

Arsenal came second in the league and reached the FA Cup final in the late 1920s, and confidence was building as the big manager from Yorkshire installed the revolutionary 'WM' formation in the 1930s. This innovative attacking shape helped Arsenal become the best team English football had ever seen.

Arsenal began the decade by winning the FA Cup in 1930, beating Huddersfield 2–0 in the final. The following season the Gunners won the title for the first time, scoring an incredible 127 goals in the process. Two seasons later Arsenal won the championship again, scoring 118 goals, and were on the verge of retaining their title when Chapman died suddenly of pneumonia in January 1934. Aged just 55, Herbert Chapman left a widow, a daughter and two sons – and a sporting legacy that would never be forgotten.

As *The Times* put it in his obituary, Chapman had been determined to make the game of football "attractive to the shilling-paying public". He had the club construct new, comfortable East and West Stands at Highbury, attempted to introduce spectator-friendly white footballs, installed floodlights (which the FA made him take down again – they weren't ready for them yet), introduced numbers on the back of players' shirts, and placed a giant clock at the south side of Highbury – at what became the Clock End. With these innovations, Chapman was well before his time. He also demanded that diet and fitness levels were monitored, he conceived the idea of rubber studs for use on hard pitches, and was the first manager to employ physios to help players recover from injuries.

Other Chapman innovations are still evident today: managers leading the teams on to the field at the FA Cup final; Arsenal's famous red shirts with white sleeves; and the tube station 'Arsenal', which he persuaded London Underground to change from 'Gillespie Road'. Chapman also set management milestones by being the first real player-manager while at Northampton and becoming the first professional manager of the England team for a match against Italy in Rome in 1933.

The clock that Chapman had installed in Highbury now stands at the Emirates Stadium, as does the Jacob Epstein sculpture of the Yorkshireman that formerly sat in the old stadium's Marble

Halls. Herbert Chapman was inducted into English Football's Hall of Fame in 2003, and an English Heritage Blue Plaque resides at the address in Hendon, north London, where Chapman lived as Arsenal manager. Overall, his career – as *The Times* reported on his death – was so successful and innovative that "a novelist would reject it as too far-fetched".

Name Herbert Chapman
Born Sheffield, Yorkshire, January 19th 1878
Died January 6th 1934
Arsenal manager 1925–34
Arsenal honours League Championship (1930/31, 1932/33), FA Cup (1930)

— TV GOONERS —

(Lee) Dixon of Dock Green
(Charlie) George and Mildred
The (Liam) Brady Bunch
Alas (Alan) Smith and (Charles) Jones
The (Willie) Young Ones
The (David) Price Is Right
Crown (David) Court
King of the (Colin) Hill
The Canon and (Alan) Ball Show
The (Tony) Addams Family

— POLITICAL GUNNERS —

In between revolutions, debates and speeches, even these politicians like to unwind with a bit of Spurs-hating:

Fidel Castro
Aleksander Kwasniewski (Polish president, 1995–2005)
(Baron) Brian Mawhinney (former Conservative cabinet minister, now chairman of the Football League)
Sir Trevor Phillips, chairman of the Commission for Racial Equality
(Baron) Chris Smith (former Labour MP)

— HIDDEN TREASURES —

When the Emirates Stadium was being built, the club decided to create a 'time capsule' of Gunners goodies to bequeath to future generations. Club officials chose 15 items to be buried beneath the stadium, and threw open the other 25 suggestions to fans. Here's what the fans chose to include:

1. A list of all Arsenal players ever
2. Tony Adams' captain's armband
3. A piece of Highbury turf
4. Every Arsenal home shirt
5. A replica model of Highbury
6. Marble from the Marble Halls
7. An aerial picture of Highbury
8. A Highbury flag
9. A record of all matches played at Highbury
10. A picture of Ian Wright's celebration after his record-breaking goal
11. A video of the history of Arsenal from 1886 to the present
12. A history of the crest
13. A shirt signed by the squad at the time
14. A picture of all the Arsenal managers
15. Pictures of all the Arsenal captains in sequence
16. A video montage of memorable Gunners moments
17. A replica of the clock from the Clock End
18. A copy of the newspaper from the day the capsule was buried
19. A picture of the old North Bank packed with fans
20. A picture or replica of all trophies won
21. A Highbury match ticket
22. A David Rocastle shirt
23. A video providing a virtual guided tour of Highbury
24. A picture of the famous back four of the 1990s
25. The fans' message book

— BORING, BORING ARSENAL —

Ask any English football fan which team has had the reputation for being the dullest in the land, and most people will suggest Arsenal FC. Surprisingly perhaps, the Gunners reputation for a ruthlessly efficient but ever so slightly dreary style of play even pre-dates the long-ball, clean-sheet George Graham era of the 1980s and 1990s. In fact, Arsenal were boring the pants off opposition fans as far back as the 1930s. As then manager George Allison, who had a small role in the 1939 film *The Arsenal Stadium Mystery*, put it: "It's 1–0 to the Arsenal, that's how we like it".

Both Herbert Chapman's and, later, Allison's Arsenal sides liked to sit back before catching teams on the break through a pass from playmaker Alex James. The negative style frustrated opposing supporters, as did that of the championship-winning team of 1947/48 under Tom Whittaker, whose strength lay firmly in defence.

Among contemporary fans, however, Arsenal's reputation for nicking a goal and then holding on to it thanks to a miserly defence mainly stems from George Graham's side of the late 1980s and early 1990s. Once they went a goal up, the Arsenal back four of Lee Dixon, Steve Bould, Tony Adams and Nigel Winterburn would then hold firm in the tackle, and make effective use of the offside trap to reduce the opposition's attacking threat. Indeed, this tactic became so famous it was referred to in the 1997 film *The Full Monty* when four characters practicing a dance routine were instructed to move forward and put their hands in the air in unison, as if claiming offside.

Of course, Arsenal had some players at this time – including Brian Marwood, Paul Merson, David Rocastle and Anders Limpar – who could all light up a match with a bit of magic. But many fans – especially opposition ones – would agree that few Arsenal matches during the Graham years were end-to-end classics. His team, however, was very successful. Ian Wright's arrival, especially, meant there was a top-class, prolific goalscorer to be relied upon to get the one, and the rock-solid defence was there to secure the nil.

Arsenal's 1994 Cup Winners' Cup final triumph over hot favourites Parma was a prime example. An Alan Smith volley and some heroic defending meant millions of TV viewers around Europe were introduced to the chant '1–0 to the Arsenal'.

Nowadays, of course, the chant of 'boring, boring Arsenal' that used to come from rival fans has been sung lovingly and ironically by Gunners supporters since Arsene Wenger's arrival, as the team have consistently played some of the Premiership's – and, possibly, even Europe's – most attractive football.

— EARTH ELEVEN —

Arsenal are the first club to have fielded 11 players of different nationality in the same Champions League game. When Englishman Justin Hoyte replaced Kolo Toure in the 28th minute of the 2–1 win over Hamburg on September 13th 2006, he helped to create European football history. The Gunners line-up at that stage read:

Jens Lehmann (Germany)
Emmanuel Eboue (Ivory Coast)
Johan Djourou (Switzerland)
Justin Hoyte (England)
William Gallas (France)
Tomas Rosicky (Czech Republic)
Gilberto (Brazil)
Cesc Fabregas (Spain)
Alexander Hleb (Belarus)
Emmanuel Adebayor (Togo)
Robin van Persie (Holland)

Fulham had already fielded a Global XI in the domestic English game when they beat Bury 3–1 in the League Cup in 2002.

— THEIR NAMES LIVE ON —

The following Gunners lost their lives while serving in the Armed Forces during the Second World War:

Henry Cook
Bobby Daniel
William Dean
Hugh Glass
Leslie Lack
William Parr
Sidney Pugh
Herbie Roberts
Cyril Tooze

— CURTAIN RAISERS—

In 19 appearances in the FA Community Shield (formerly the Charity Shield), Arsenal have come out on top 12 times. This is second to only joint record-holders Manchester United and Liverpool who have won it 13 times each to date. The Red Devils have failed to beat the Gunners in five curtain-raisers in open play, with the Gunners winning three and losing the other two on penalties. Arsenal have shared the trophy once – with FA Cup-holders Tottenham Hotspur in 1991. Arsenal's best decade in the competition was the 1930s, when they won five times in seven Charity Shield matches.

FA Charity Shield
1930 Arsenal 2–1 Sheffield Wednesday
1931 Arsenal 1–0 West Bromwich Albion
1933 Arsenal 3–0 Everton
1934 Arsenal 4–0 Manchester City
1935 Sheffield Wednesday 1–0 Arsenal
1936 Sunderland 2–0 Arsenal
1938 Arsenal 2–1 Preston North End
1948 Arsenal 4–3 Manchester United
1953 Arsenal 3–1 Blackpool
1979 Liverpool 3–1 Arsenal
1989 Liverpool 1–0 Arsenal
1991 Arsenal 0–0 Tottenham Hotspur (Shield shared)
1993 Manchester United 1–1 Arsenal (Manchester United won 5–4 on penalties)
1998 Arsenal 3–0 Manchester United
1999 Arsenal 2–1 Manchester United

FA Community Shield
2002 Arsenal 1–0 Liverpool
2003 Manchester United 1–1 Arsenal (Manchester United won 4–3 on penalties)
2004 Arsenal 3–1 Manchester United
2005 Chelsea 2–1 Arsenal

— GUNNERS LEGENDS: ARSENE WENGER —

Arsene who?

When *We Love You Arsenal: The Official Album* came out in 2005, it opened with a number called 'The Arsene Wenger Chorus'. The song featured the words 'Ar-sene Wen-ger' sung to the tune of Handel's 'Hallelujah' – a piece of music that was written, of course, to celebrate the coming of the Messiah. Without stretching the analogy too far, it could be said that Arsenal found their own spiritual saviour in the figure of the intellectual-looking Frenchman, who arrived at Highbury from Japanese club Nagoya Grampus Eight in 1996.

At the time, Wenger's appointment was a big shock, with the

Evening Standard newspaper famously proclaiming 'Arsene Who?' on its back page. Most fans expected Arsenal to appoint another British or Irish manager in the mould of former boss George Graham. Followers of Japanese or French football might have heard of him, but in Islington confusion reigned. However, the negative headlines soon faded from memory, as Wenger immediately changed Arsenal for the better with new signings like Patrick Vieira and Nicolas Anelka, a revolutionary fitness and diet regime, and a complete tactical overhaul.

Wenger has made it his speciality to find young players at clubs around the world and whisk them off cheaply to Arsenal before their previous employers even knew what talent they had. He's done this regularly with footballers such as Anelka, Kolo Toure and Cesc Fabregas. The board loved Wenger for his business sense – he bought Anelka, for example, for £500,000 from Paris Saint Germain and sold him two years later for £22.5m. As with Vieira, the manager rescued Thierry Henry from a miserable time in Italy; he extended the careers of Arsenal's legendary back four of Lee Dixon, Tony Adams, Steve Bould and Nigel Winterburn, and he got the best out of Dennis Bergkamp. The players left the pies and pints behind to become super athletes, but what was most startling to not just Arsenal fans, but football fans the world over, was that Wenger helped end Arsenal's 'boring' reputation.

Under George Graham the Gunners were known for grinding out dull 1–0 victories. Wenger's approach was completely at odds with this win at all costs ethos. Of course, he wanted his side to win, but he demanded that they also play attractive, passing football. Over time, Arsenal's style of play became the model for pass-and-move football the world over. There were no more long balls, barely even punts from the goalkeeper. Wenger instructed his side to send the ball short to the full-backs, who would in turn find a central midfielder dropping deep. When it all clicked, a series of diagonal runs and short passes would follow, bamboozling the opposition, and the move would end with someone like Freddie Ljungberg joyfully passing the ball into the back of the net.

For his achievements and qualities as a coach, Arsene Wenger is the greatest manager the club has ever had, surpassing even the great 1930s visionary Herbert Chapman. To date, 'Le Professeur' has won three League Championships and four FA Cups and taken

Arsenal to a first Champions League final. He has won the Manager of the Year award three times, twice after winning the Double with Arsenal in 1997/98 and 2001/02, and once after guiding his team through an entire Premiership season unbeaten, in 2003/04.

Wenger, who speaks six languages, has received the Legion of Honour from France, an honourary OBE from Britain, the Freedom of Islington and a place in the English Football Hall of Fame. Such is the belief in Wenger among both the fans – whose 'Arsene Knows' banners fly proudly in the ground – and the board, that he was given remit to assist in the design of Arsenal's new stadium. The Gunners moved into Wenger's dream, the Emirates Stadium in Ashburton Grove, for the start of the 2006/07 season, as Highbury and the past were left behind.

Name Arsene Wenger
Nickname Le Professeur
Born Strasbourg, France, October 22nd 1949
Arsenal manager 1996–
Arsenal honours League Championship and FA Cup Double (1997/98, 2001/02), League Championship (2003/04), FA Cup (2003, 2005)

— THE ALL ENGLAND CLUB —

Arsenal underwent an epic change during the 1990–2000 decade, going from being a successful team of Englishmen, to becoming an equally successful team of overseas players. The last time Arsenal fielded an entirely English line-up was back on April 19th 1994 for a 1–1 home draw with Wimbledon. This was the starting XI:

1. David Seaman
2. Lee Dixon
3. Martin Keown
4. Tony Adams
5. Steve Bould
6. Paul Davis
7. Ray Parlour
8. Ian Selley
9. Ian Wright
10. Alan Smith
11. Kevin Campbell

— GEORGE GRAHAM'S BACK FOUR —

Arsenal had the most respected defence in the land under manager George Graham, and successors Bruce Rioch and Arsene Wenger also made good use of the same mean back line.

Left back Nigel Winterburn and right back Lee Dixon were signed by Graham in 1987 and 1988 respectively, both staying at the club until the new millennium. Their consistency throughout this time was remarkable, and both won England caps – athletic, sure-footed Dixon being a regular for his country, while dogged Winterburn was unlucky to feature in the same England era as the legendary Stuart Pearce. The back four was completed by centre half and skipper Tony Adams, and his partner in central defence Steve Bould.

Between them the quartet made 2,201 appearances for Arsenal (Adams 669, Dixon 619, Winterburn 584 and Bould 329). In the years during their reign at Highbury, Arsenal's goals-against column featured some very low figures indeed (see below), with a then club record of just 18 goals against during the 1990/91 championship-winning season. Significantly, Bould, Dixon and Winterburn were all ever-present in that campaign. Remarkably, in 1998/99, they went one better, conceding just 17 goals in their final season together.

The 'Fab Four's' effectiveness was founded on constant practice in training, especially the repetition of defensive drills. George Graham used to take his four defenders to one side during training sessions, concentrating on their organisation for the offside trap, and their understanding of how to cover for each other when opposition attackers made runs towards goal. Graham also used his back four in certain attacking situations. For example, the towering 6ft 4in Bould became an expert at flicking on corners at the near post, Dixon's calmness under pressure made him Arsenal's main penalty-taker for a time, while the powerful Adams collected 49 (mostly headed) career goals for the club.

The quartet's finest hour, though, came in the 1–0 victory in the 1994 European Cup Winners' Cup Final over Parma. The Italian side fielded three world-class strikers in Faustino Asprilla, Tomas Brolin and Gianfranco Zola – all of whom were marked out of the game by Adams and co as Arsenal kept a clean sheet. Steve Bould picked up the Man of the Match award, but it might just as easily have gone to any of his other three defensive colleagues.

Season	League goals conceded
1988/89	36
1989/90	38
1990/91	18
1991/92	46
1992/93	38
1993/94	28
1994/95	49
1995/96	32
1996/97	32
1997/98	33
1998/99	17

— LEATHER ON WILLOW —

Three cricket matches were played at Highbury during its 93 years of existence. They were benefit matches in the 1940s and 1950s for players Denis and Leslie Compton, and Jack Young. Each involved an Arsenal XI taking on Middlesex at cricket.

Arsenal had an outstanding relationship with cricket until the late 1950s, with several of the club's players playing top-level cricket as well as football. Arthur Milton was the last Gunner to represent England at both football and cricket – he was a midfielder for Arsenal, winning the title in 1952/53, but also excelled for Gloucestershire. Wally Hardinge was the first Arsenal man to be selected by his country in both sports, in the late 1910s and early 1920s. *Wisden* Cricketer of the Year in 1915, he played for Kent.

Most famous of all, however, were Compton brothers Denis and Leslie, who were top class in both sports. Leslie was a wicketkeeper for Middlesex, but was an even better footballer. Younger sibling Denis – known as the 'Brylcreem Boy' following his endorsement of the hair product – became Middlesex captain and a cricketing legend, having a stand named after him at Lord's. He was also a fine footballer, winning the league (1948) and the FA Cup (1950) with the Gunners.

— ARSENAL UP, TOTTENHAM DOWN —

Even to this day Tottenham fans complain about Arsenal's promotion to the First Division at their expense in 1919 – and, it has to be said, the circumstances of the Gunners ascent were pretty odd.

In 1914/15, the last season before football was put on hold for the duration of the First World War, Arsenal finished a disappointing fifth in the Second Division. Yet, when the first post-war season kicked off, the Gunners were in the First Division – and, as every Arsenal fan knows, they have stayed in the top flight ever since. Nearly a century on, the story of how Arsenal gained promotion is still shrouded in some mystery but there's no doubt about the key figure in the drama – the Gunners chairman and 'Mr Fixit', Sir Henry Norris.

Before the start of the 1919/20 campaign, with football re-starting following the First World War, the Football League voted to enlarge the First Division from 20 to 22 teams. Logically, Spurs and Chelsea, the two bottom clubs when the last official season ended, should have stayed up. And the two top teams from the Second Division, Derby and Preston should have been promoted. Sir Henry, though, had other ideas. The wealthy knight, Tory MP, former Mayor of Fulham and property magnate used his influence to press Arsenal's cause – and is rumoured also to have slipped a few notes into a few pockets – when the matter was discussed at the League's AGM.

Norris's close friend, the Football League President 'Honest' John McKenna, spoke in Arsenal's favour at the meeting, declaring that the Gunners deserved Tottenham's place in the top flight because they had been in the League for 15 years longer than their close neighbours. The representatives of Barnsley and Wolves – who had finished third and fourth respectively in the Second Division – naturally disagreed, but McKenna won the day. In the vote to decide the last First Division place, Arsenal received 18 votes, compared to eight for Spurs, five for Barnsley and a smattering for some other clubs. Arsenal were up, Tottenham were down, and the long rivalry between the two clubs was given its first dramatic twist.

— GUNNERS LEGENDS: LIAM BRADY —

Liam 'Chippy' Brady

Liam Brady is one of those players who would have been guaranteed a place in any team – luckily for Highbury, for six seasons that team was Arsenal. The stylish Irishman conjured goals and trickery for a Gunners side that otherwise was rather lacking in inspiration, helping the club win the FA Cup in 1979 before leaving for Juventus two years later.

Discovered at the tender age of 13 in Ireland, Brady came to Arsenal as part of the 'Green Gunners' revolution that brought fellow stars Frank Stapleton and David O'Leary to the club, as well as manager Terry Neill. A consistent performer, Brady was the creative hub of a Gunners side that challenged for major honours at home and abroad.

As well as making countless assists, Brady was also a regular scorer. His famous goal at White Hart Lane in a 5–0 demolition of Tottenham in December 1978 is still recalled by many older Arsenal fans. Winning the ball from Peter Taylor in midfield, Brady moved forward from the left towards the edge of the area, before unleashing a cannonball with his favoured left foot that suddenly swung its way into the top right-hand corner.

Brady was voted Arsenal's Player of the Year three times, and PFA Player's Player of the Year in 1979. His deft and accurate passing was greatly appreciated by strikers Malcolm Macdonald and Frank Stapleton in the late 1970s, and he was the inspiration for Arsenal central midfielders to come, such as Paul Davis and Michael Thomas. Throughout his career he lived up to the memorable assessment of an Arsenal scout that the young Brady's left foot was so sweet, "it practically talks".

Brady's highlight with Arsenal was winning the FA Cup in 1979, after setting up Alan Sunderland's dramatic late winner in the 3–2 win against Manchester United at Wembley. He tasted defeat in two other FA Cup Finals in 1978 and 1980 and, also in 1980, missed a penalty in the European Cup Winners' Cup final shoot-out defeat to Valencia.

Brady left Arsenal aged only 24 to become one of Italian football's most successful foreign imports with Juventus, before returning to play out his career at West Ham United. After a spell managing Celtic, he returned to Arsenal as head of the youth set-up. If he can unearth and bring through anyone half as talented as himself, the Emirates Stadium is on to a winner.

Name Liam Brady
Nickname Chippy
Born Dublin, Ireland, February 13th 1956
Arsenal appearances 294
Arsenal goals 59
International appearances Republic of Ireland, 72
International goals 9

ARSENAL
Home Kits
1886-2008

www.historicalkits.co.uk

1886-90
(Dial Square/Royal Arsenal)

1894-95
(Woolwich Arsenal)

1895-96
(Woolwich Arsenal)

1896-97
(Woolwich Arsenal)

1897-1900
(Woolwich Arsenal)

1905-06
(Woolwich Arsenal)

1906-07
(Woolwich Arsenal)

1907-08
(Woolwich Arsenal)

1908-14
Woolwich Arsenal

1919-20

1920-29

1929-30

1930-31

1931-32

1932-33

1933-34

1934-35

1935-39

1945-46

1946-58

1958-61

1962-63

1963-64

1964-66

1966-67

1967-69

1969-78

1978-81

1981-82

1982-83

1983-84

1984-86

1986-88

1988-90

1990-92

1992-94

1994-96

1996-98

1998-99

1999-2000

2000-02   **2002-04**   **2004-05**   **2005-06**

2006-08

— EMIRATES STATS —

Arguably Britain's most spectacular football club stadium, Arsenal's Emirates ground in Ashburton Grove, north London is an engineering and design marvel. Here are some concrete Emirates facts:

- The 60,432-capacity stadium took only 123 weeks and two days to build.
- The seating breakdown is:

    26,646 fans in the upper tier

    24,425 fans in the lower tier

    7,139 at Club Level

    2,222 at Box Level (including 128 seats in the Directors' Box and 168 in the Diamond Club)

    80 seats in the two dugout areas

    Away fans get allocated between 1,500 and 9,000 seats per game
- The entire complex covers 17 acres.
- There were 1,400 construction workers building the stadium during its busiest period – with 9,000 people involved in creating the Emirates overall. It would have taken one person 685 years non-stop to do it on their own. If he or she had been allowed to work normal hours, the Emirates would not have been completed until around the year 4006.
- Access for all. There are 500 spaces for disabled fans.
- More than one million fans are likely to attend matches at the ground each season.
- The internal floor space covers 91,172m sq, which is almost the size of the Millennium Dome. The stadium measures 246m North-South by 200m East-West.
- The stadium rises up 41m above pitch level.
- Glazing used at the Emirates adds up to 15,000m sq.
- The 5,100 tonne-load roof can support up to 25cm deep snow across its 27,200m sq area.
- Fans can expect to receive 100,000 food and drink orders at each game, from 250 outlets.
- Four pints of beer can be handed over every five seconds – that's 2,400 pints a minute across the stadium.
- There is 105m by 68m worth of pitch on which to view Arsenal games at the Emirates, while action replays and

additional information can be seen on the two giant 72m sq Mitsubishi screens. The movie *My Big Fat Greek Wedding* was used to test the screens, while the sound system first ran dance tune 'Encore Une Fois' by Sash.

— FUNDRAISING TARGETS—

Arsenal were not always the 'Bank of England' club. Before Henry Norris got involved with the Gunners, taking them to their new stadium north of the river at Highbury, Woolwich Arsenal needed every penny they could get. And as such, in 1902 the club held an archery competition on Plumstead Common as a fund-raiser to buy new players.

Amazingly, the plan paid off as a whopping £1,200 was raised, and the Gunners were able to spend the proceeds on penalty-taking expert Jimmy Bellamy, as well as Tommy Shanks who would go on to represent Ireland.

— ARSENAL HORDES —

Arsenal is officially the best-supported football club in the world by membership. There are currently 175,000 people registered with Arsenal as members – that is significantly more than second-placed club Benfica of Portugal, who have 161,000. Arsenal estimate that they have 27 million fans worldwide, which puts the Gunners third on the planet in terms of non-member support.

Things look promising for the future, as the club has three times as many members as can fit into the Emirates – the stadium was full to its capacity of 60,000 for most of its inaugural 2006/07 season. And of the 175,000 fans signed up with the club, 29,000 are Junior Gunners – which makes the scheme for youngsters the most successful in British football. Seven Arsenal staff members are employed just to deal with the Junior Gunners.

Arsenal also have approximately 90 official supporters' clubs around the world, and employ a liaison officer at Arsenal HQ to work with them.

— ARSENAL TUBE STATION —

Arsenal remains the only football club in London to have a tube station named after it.

Re-naming Gillespie Road station was the brainwave of Herbert Chapman, the Gunners' visionary manager of the 1920s and 1930s credited with turning Arsenal in the world's best team of the era, and inventing many new aspects of the game that are routine today.

The idea first came to Chapman when he visited the club as manager of Leeds City in 1913, and was astounded by how close the tube station was to Arsenal's stadium. Such was Chapman's standing in the game that – having taken Huddersfield Town to three successive League Championship victories in the 1920s, and then taking charge of top team Arsenal – his proposal was passed during a meeting with the London Electric Railway in 1932.

"Whoever heard of Gillespie Road?" he pointedly asked, referring to the station's existing name. "It's Arsenal around here."

LER initially recommended a compromise of 'Highbury Hill', fearing an avalanche of requests from the other London clubs, but Chapman's powers of persuasion won the day. The LER's decision to change the name of the station was the culmination of months of lobbying and cost the company a lot of money, as machinery had to be altered, along with thousands of signs, maps, timetables, and tickets. It was a big task for the London Underground company, but Chapman argued that it would be worth their while by suggesting that more customers might use the station and the line if Gillespie Road was renamed Arsenal. The new station was born on November 5th 1932.

— SICK AS A PARROT —

After Tottenham Hotspur made a tour of South America in 1908, they were presented with a parrot by the captain of the ship they travelled on.

The parrot was brought back to White Hart Lane where it perched happily for 11 years until it keeled over and died on the very day that Spurs lost their place in the First Division to Arsenal in March 1919 (see *Arsenal Up, Tottenham Down*, page 54.)

It is believed that this is where perhaps the greatest football cliché of all, 'sick as a parrot', originated.

— HIGHBURY'S LEGACY —

After 93 years and 2,010 Arsenal matches, the beloved old stadium of Highbury was finally decommissioned in 2006. As the football club left for the new ground down the road, the old ground was left behind and eventually turned into 711 residential flats.

Highbury's art deco East Stand, designed by Claude Waterlow Ferrier and William Binnie from 1932–36, is a Grade II listed building, and as such had to be converted rather than replaced. The West Stand was also turned into apartments, but the old North Bank and Clock End are gone, with purpose-built facilities in their place. The pitch is now a two-acre communal garden, its paths replicating the old markings.

The redevelopment of the stadium – the first of its kind in the world – proved to be a goldmine for Arsenal. With the prices of flats originally starting at £230,000 and rising to £325,000, the total income to the club may well top the £300m mark.

The communal facilities for the one, two and three bedroom apartments include a fitness centre with swimming pool, underground parking, 24-hour concierge and, of course, garden access.

Former midfielder Robert Pires is among those whose address now reads 'The Stadium, Highbury Square'. The Frenchman, who scored his 84th Arsenal goal during the last game at Highbury in May 2006, explained that "buying a flat in Highbury is a symbol of my affection for the club. To have a flat on the ground where I once played, which holds so many fond memories for me, is something very special."

— CENTENARY CELEBRATIONS —

Arsenal celebrated their centenary on December 27th 1986 by beating Southampton at Highbury to maintain their position at the top of the old First Division. Among the former players attending the match were legendary skipper Joe Mercer, prolific striker Ted Drake and George Male, the last survivor of the powerful Arsenal side of the early 1930s.

Niall Quinn scored the only goal of the game to give the final score a familiar look – 1–0 to the Arsenal!

— THE FRENCH CONNECTION —

Arsene Wenger's reign as manager of Arsenal began in 1996 with the signing of two Frenchmen, Remi Garde and Patrick Vieira. This ushered in a French revolution at the London club, where 16 Gallic players in total have been brought in to date. Including the brief stay of replacement keeper Guillaume Warmuz who was signed from Lens, the Gunners could come up with an entire French team from the Wenger era:

Guillaume Warmuz

Abou Diaby   William Gallas   Pascal Cygan   Gael Clichy

Sylvian Wiltord   Emmanuel Petit   Patrick Vieira   Robert Pires

Thierry Henry   Nicolas Anelka

Subs: David Grondin, Gilles Grimandi, Mathieu Flamini, Remi Garde, Jeremie Aliadiere

— HOME SWEET HOME —

After the Gunners finally left Highbury in 2006, their fans could look back on cheering on more than 1,000 victories in over 2,000 matches at the ground. It wasn't always 1–0 to the Arsenal, as the team averaged a 2–1 victory in games there between 1913 and 2006, with around 4,000 goals scored and 2,000 conceded in total. The Gunners were only beaten on home turf 339 times in those 93 years – and hope it will be more like 200 years before they reach that total at the Emirates Stadium. Here's the complete record:

Competition	Played	Won	Drawn	Lost	For	Against
League	1,689	981	412	296	3,372	1,692
FA Cup	142	92	32	18	305	123
League Cup	98	69	14	15	195	74
Europe	76	50	17	9	153	60
Charity Shield	5	4	0	1	13	6
Total	2,010	1,196	475	339	4,038	1,955

—WALCOTT THE BOY WONDER —

When Theo Walcott curled a shot around Chelsea's Petr Cech in the 2007 Carling Cup final, he became the second youngest player ever to score in the final of the competition.

A year earlier, Arsenal had made Walcott the most expensive 16-year-old in British football history when they signed him from Southampton for up to £12.5m, depending on appearances. Walcott rewarded them with assists in his Premiership and Champions League debuts for the Gunners, and eventually grabbed his first strike for his new club in the all-London final at Cardiff's Millennium Stadium on Feburary 25th 2007.

The wonderkid, nicknamed 'The Newbury Express' – he's so fast that former boss Harry Redknapp says "he can run through puddles and not make a splash" – started and finished the move himself. Retrieving the ball from a corner, Walcott turned past two Chelsea players before swapping passes with Abou Diaby and delivering a swerving a shot high into goalkeeper Cech's net.

Walcott had previously become England's youngest-ever player – aged 17 years and 75 days – when he turned out against Hungary, before being picked for Sven-Goran Eriksson's squad to the 2006 World Cup in Germany.

— IT'S A DEAL, IT'S A STEAL —

Arsenal have long had an eye for a bargain, as the following list shows:

Eddie Hapgood: £950
George Graham: £50,000 plus Tommy Baldwin, from Chelsea
Pat Jennings: £45,000
John Hollins: £75,000
Perry Groves: £75,000
Nigel Winterburn: £350,000
Lee Dixon: £400,000
Steve Bould: £390,000
Patrick Vieira: £3m
Nicholas Anelka: £500,000

— COOL KEEPERS —

Arsenal have had many wonderful goalkeepers. Bob Wilson, Pat Jennings and David Seaman stand out in recent times, but the club's great goalkeeping history goes back even further to the start of the last century.

Liverpudlian goalie Jimmy Ashcroft became the first Arsenal player to win an England cap, after he signed for the then Woolwich-based team in 1900. He kept 17 clean sheets in 24 matches during the 1901/02 season – an achievement that has never been bettered in English football, and took 96 years to match when another Arsenal keeper, Alex Manninger, did it in 1997/98. By the end of the 1904/05 season Ashcroft had set another record of appearing in 154 consecutive matches, a feat which was eventually surpassed by Tom Parker 25 years later.

The great goalie under Herbert Chapman was Frank Moss, who was a fine performer between the sticks as Arsenal ran rampant in the 1930s. Moss won the League Championship three times with the Gunners, and even scored once when he was moved to the left wing having dislocated his shoulder. The courageous and acrobatic Jack Kelsey was next big Highbury hero in goal, the gigantic Welshman winning the title in 1952/53 and reaching the quarter-finals of the 1958 World Cup with his country.

Twenty years later, the much-loved Bob Wilson won plaudits and silverware during his spell with Arsenal in the late 1960s and early 1970s. An immensely brave keeper who was known for diving at the feet of onrushing opponents and never wearing gloves, Wilson was Arsenal's Player of the Year in the 1970/71 Double season. In total, Scottish international Wilson made 308 appearances for the Gunners, before becoming the club's goalkeeping coach for much of the next 30 years.

Pat Jennings had eight glorious seasons and played in four cup finals for Arsenal, his huge hands and immense aura making him a firm favourite among Gooners. The Northern Irishman, who played for Spurs either side of his Highbury career, also won a record 119 caps for his country.

John Lukic was a big hit on the North Bank in the 1980s, winning a League Cup medal and the championship in 1988/89, but it was his successor David Seaman who became arguably Arsenal's all-time greatest keeper. The enormous Yorkshireman with the moustache – and, later in his career, much-mocked ponytail – was signed from QPR in 1990 for a world record fee of £1.3m. The fee proved to be a bargain as Seamo's Arsenal career lasted for 13 years. 'Safe Hands', as he was dubbed, was a world-class keeper for both club and country, helping both Arsenal and England to victories in crucial penalty shoot-outs. His medal haul was also rather impressive: three league titles, four FA Cups, one League Cup and one European Cup Winners' Cup.

With Arsenal's loveably eccentric German keeper Jens Lehmann more recently to be found between the sticks, the great Gunners goalie tradition looks set to continue.

— CAPTAINS MARVEL —

Perhaps more than any other club, Arsenal have been blessed with many truly great captains.

Tom Parker lifted the club's first trophy, the 1930 FA Cup, having previously set an appearance record that still hasn't been broken. The right back from Southampton was ever-present for more than three years – a total of 172 matches. His place as captain was taken by multi-talented Scottish playmaker Alex James and then Eddie Hapgood, who became Arsenal's first truly inspirational captain.

Hapgood began his working life as a milkman in Bristol, playing a bit of football for non-league Kettering Town. Amazingly, he ended the 1930s as one of the all-time Arsenal greats, a club and national captain who won an incredible five League championships with the Gunners. The left back owed his incredible transformation to Herbert Chapman, the manager who paid £950 for his services in 1927 and turned him into arguably the best player in his position in the world.

Hapgood was one of a record seven Arsenal players who appeared against Italy in November 1934, breaking his nose in the infamous 'Battle of Highbury'. Four years later, in Berlin, he was outraged when he was forced to give the Nazi salute before his England side famously battered Germany 6–3.

Highbury's next super skipper was possibly Arsenal's best ever, although Frank McLintock and Tony Adams in years to come would have something to say about that. Joe Mercer was an experienced defender who had won the title with Everton when he joined the Gunners in 1946. He steered Arsenal to League titles in 1947/48 and 1952/53, the latter when he was almost 40 years old. The FA Cup win over Liverpool in 1950 was an emotional occasion for Mercer, as he triumphed over the players he trained with every day – at the time he was running a grocery business in Merseyside and commuting down to London for matches.

After the Gunners narrowly lost in the 1952 FA Cup Final against Newcastle, Mercer famously said: "I thought the greatest honour was captaining England. It isn't – it was captaining Arsenal today."

1960s skipper George Eastham was in England's 1966 World Cup-winning squad, and won plaudits for his astute passing at Highbury. He was also instrumental in modernising the transfer system, having taken on the football authorities and his former club Newcastle in the High Court in 1963 over his right to a transfer once his contract ran out.

Eastham's replacement was Arsenal legend Frank McLintock, the Scottish central defender who lifted Arsenal's first European trophy in 1970 and, the following year, the club's first Double (see *Arsenal Legends: Frank McLintock*, page 37).

Arsene Wenger's assistant manager Pat Rice, a Double winner and Irish international full-back, became skipper after McLintock. He was followed by England's regular left-back of the 1980s, Kenny Sansom. Eyebrows were raised when Gunners boss George Graham passed the skipper's armband to a 21-year-old lad named Tony Adams in 1988. But Adams went on to become a general at the heart of the Arsenal defence, winning three titles and a host of other honours, in a wonderful Highbury career spanning three decades (see *Arsenal Legends: Tony Adams*, page 103).

Following Adams' retirement, two sublimely skilful Arsenal players took over captaincy duties. Both World Cup winners with France, first Patrick Vieira and then Thierry Henry became Arsene Wenger's leaders on the pitch. Vieira's legendary passion, power and touch in central midfield helped him to inspire his side to two FA Cup wins and the unbeaten Premiership campaign of 2003/04. After his departure, global superstar Thierry Henry took Arsenal to their first Champions League final in 2006, the team narrowly losing to Barcelona. Thierry finally passed on the armband to his successor Gilberto, the Brazilian World Cup winner, after moving to Barcelona in the summer of 2007.

— GREAT ARSENAL MOMENTS AT
WHITE HART LANE —

1. **Winning the league in 1971.** Ray Kennedy scored the winner, and Bob Wilson held on in goal to secure the first part of the Double.
2. **Winning the league again in 2004.** Goals from Patrick Vieira and Robert Pires put Arsenal on the way to a second title-clincher on Spurs turf.
3. **David Rocastle's winner in the League Cup semi-final replay in 1987.** When Rocky's shot hit the back of the net, it was the third time Arsenal had won at White Hart Lane in one season. The red-and-white side of north London went on to taste success in the final.
4. **The League Cup semi-final fight-back sparked by Julio 'The Beast' Baptista in 2007.** The Brazilian attacker worked wonders at the Lane to draw the Gunners level, after Tottenham led 2–0 at half-time against Arsenal's youngsters. The Gunners won the second leg 3–1 to book a place in the final against Chelsea at the Millennium stadium.
5. **The Gunners triumph in a nine-goal thriller.** On November 13th 2004, Tottenham and Arsenal fought out the most astonishing north London derby ever. The match finished 5–4 to Arsenal, with all the goals being scored by different players. Robert Pires, again, scored the goal that was the difference between the sides. A satisfying trip up the Seven Sisters Road for the Arsenal.

— EMIRATES INTERNATIONALS —

Prior to the start of the 2007/08 season Arsenal's new stadium had played host to two international fixtures, both involving Brazil. On September 3rd 2006 Kaka and co entertained fellow South American giants Argentina in north London, winning 3–0.

Two months later, on February 6th 2007, the Emirates again reverberated to the sound of samba rhythms as Brazil took on Portugal in another high profile friendly. Thanks to goals by Simao and Chelsea's Ricardo Carvalho, Portugal won 2–0.

— LITERALLY SPEAKING —

A list of Gunners who have revealed all (or nearly all) in their autobiographies:

Tony Adams: *Addicted*
George Allison: *Allison Calling*
Alan Ball: *Playing Extra Time*
Cliff Bastin: *Cliff Bastin Remembers*
Liam Brady: *So Far So Good*
Charlie George: *My Story*
George Graham: *The Glory And The Grief*
Perry Groves: *We All Live In A Perry Groves World*
Eddie Hapgood: *Football Ambassador*
David Jack: *Soccer*
Tommy Lawton: *My 20 Years Of Soccer*
Malcolm Macdonald: *An Autobiography*
Frank McLintock: *True Grit*
Paul Merson: *Rock Bottom*
Terry Neill: *Revelations Of A Football Manager*
David O'Leary: *My Story*
Robert Pires: *Footballeur*
Kenny Sansom: *Going Great Guns*
David Seaman: *Safe Hands*
Derek Tapscott: *Tappy*
Patrick Vieira: *My Autobiography*
Bob Wall: *Arsenal From The Heart*
Bob Wilson: *You've Got To Be Crazy*
Ian Wright: *Mr Wright*

— OUT OF AFRICA —

At the time of writing, Arsenal have had 15 African players from nine countries representing the club. This is more than any other English football club. Strikers Kanu of Nigeria and Togo's Emmanuel Adebayor are among the most celebrated, along with defenders Lauren from Cameroon, and Ivory Coast pair Emmanuel Eboue and Kolo Toure.

— ATTENDANCE RECORDS —

When Arsenal were at their first great peak in the 1930s, more than 70,000 people would often turn up at Highbury to cheer them on. This kind of figure was not seen again until the 1990s, when Arsenal used Wembley for their home games in the Champions League. A match at Wembley against RC Lens in the 1998/99 Champions League campaign drew a gate of 73,707 – Arsenal's largest ever.

However, this only narrowly beats the greatest ever attendance at Highbury. On March 9th 1935, 73,295 fans came to watch the Gunners draw with fellow league contenders Sunderland. That compares to a top figure of 38,419 Gooners turning up at Highbury in the modern era, with the 2003/04 game against Leicester City drawing the biggest Premiership crowd at the old stadium. The crowd record at the new Emirates stadium is 60,132 for the visit of Manchester United in January 2007.

In decades gone by, Arsenal's average attendance in a season has reflected the team's performance on the pitch, with massive highs during the League Championship winning years of 1947/48, 1952/53, 1970/71, 1988/89 and 1990/91, while the barren years in between those successes saw gates falling to as low as 23,824 in 1985/86 and 26,495 in 1975/76. The lowest league attendance at Highbury was a pitiful 4,554 for a match against Leeds United in 1966, while only 18,253 watched Arsenal v Wimbledon in the winter of 1993. During Wenger's reign at the club, however, crowds at Highbury were regularly full to bursting point, with a record 175,000 people signing up for the club's ticket membership scheme. Clearly, Highbury's limited capacity could not cope with the demand for tickets and a move to a bigger stadium became of vital importance to the club.

Average post-war league attendances at Arsenal

Season	Attendance
1946/47	43,266
1947/48	54,892
1948/49	51,478
1949/50	49,001
1950/51	50,474
1951/52	51,030
1952/53	49,141
1953/54	46,944

1954/55	43,725
1955/56	42,034
1956/57	41,093
1957/58	38,835
1958/59	45,227
1959/60	39,341
1960/61	34,318
1961/62	34,447
1962/63	32,288
1963/64	34,793
1964/65	31,327
1965/66	29,036
1966/67	31,773
1967/68	31,896
1968/69	38,423
1969/70	35,758
1970/71	43,776
1971/72	40,500
1972/73	40,246
1973/74	30,212
1974/75	28,315
1975/76	26,495
1976/77	32,671
1977/78	35,446
1978/79	36,371
1979/80	33,596
1980/81	32,480
1981/82	35,589
1982/83	24,153
1983/84	28,116
1984/85	31,205
1985/86	23,824
1986/87	29,022
1987/88	29,910
1988/89	35,593
1989/90	33,672
1990/91	37,012
1991/92	31,886
1992/93	24,403
1993/94	30,492

1994/95	35,220
1995/96	37,568
1996/97	37,821
1997/98	38,053
1998/99	38,024
1999/2000	38,033
2000/01	37,975
2001/02	38,044
2002/03	38,042
2003/04	38,079
2004/05	37,079
2005/06	38,184
2006/07	60,045

— CROSSING THE DIVIDE —

Since Arsenal moved to North London in 1913, and took Spurs' place in the First Division a few years later (see *Arsenal Up, Tottenham Down*, page 54), a massive rivalry has existed across the four miles separating the two clubs. So intense is the competition between the sides, that few players risk making the direct switch from Gunner to Lilywhite, or vice versa. However, a few brave souls have made the transition in the post-war period:

Tottenham to Arsenal
1949   Freddie Cox
1968   Jimmy Robertson
1977   Pat Jennings
1977   Steve Walford
1977   Kevin Stead
1977   Willie Young
2002   Sol Campbell

Arsenal to Tottenham
1964   Laurie Brown
1968   David Jenkins
1985   Pat Jennings
2003   Rohan Ricketts

— GUNNERS LEGENDS: THIERRY HENRY —

Va va voom!

One of the most talented players of his generation, Thierry Henry was a genuine Arsenal superstar. His jaw-dropping skill and breathtaking speed were instrumental to the club's success in recent years, while his Arsenal career has also included numerous personal highs, including being appointed club captain in 2005, the same year that he broke the Gunners' all-time scoring record.

Henry began his career at Monaco, where his manager was a certain Arsene Wenger. In 1998, aged just 20, he won the World Cup with France, playing alongside future Arsenal team-mate Emmanuel Petit. He was then snapped up by Juventus, but failed to shine out on the wing for the Italian giants. Wenger took Henry to Arsenal a year later for £10.5m, moved him into the centre of attack and, after a slow start, the young Frenchman soon became one of the most feared strikers in the Premiership.

'Terence', as he was affectionately known to the Highbury faithful, glided past defenders to score 26 goals in his first season, and 22 in his second. The following two seasons saw Henry net 32 times each, helping Arsenal win the League and FA Cup Double and another FA Cup. Then it got better.

The suave Frenchman dribbled wide, ghosted inside and slotted home 39 goals for the Gunners as they went through the entire 2003/04 season unbeaten in the league. He added another 30 and 33 strikes in the next two campaigns respectively. Thierry Henry was a phenomenon, and it wasn't just the quantity of his goals that made him so special. It was also the manner in which he scored them – with his touch, poise, elegance, vision, and above all his heart-stopping pace on the ball, Henry was truly an *artiste*. The number of assists he engineered for team-mates also made him the first name on everyone's Fantasy Football team.

With his good looks and natural charm, Henry was much in demand off the field. He appeared in some high-profile car and sports brand ads, uttering the famous 'Va-va-voom' catchphrase in an ad for Renault, and was also immortalised in cartoon form on MTV. But it was on the pitch that Thierry became a world legend. In 2000 he added the European Championship trophy to his World Cup winner's medal; he was twice voted second in FIFA's World Player of the Year awards (2003 and 2004); he was English football's Footballer of the Year a record three times (2003, 2004 and 2006) and Player's Player of the Year twice (2003 and 2004); European Golden Boot winner twice (2004 and 2005); Premiership top scorer on four occasions . . . this could go on all day. As *The Observer Sport Monthly* once observed: "Welcome to the perfect world of Thierry Henry, a footballer whom, if he didn't exist, not even a comic-book editor would dare to invent."

In the 2005/06 season, Henry cemented his position as an Arsenal legend. Installed as club captain in August after the departure of Patrick Vieira, he took Ian Wright's mantle as Arsenal's all-time top goalscorer in October. No one had ever scored 100 goals at Highbury until Henry achieved it in November against Blackburn. In February he overtook Cliff Bastin as Arsenal's top goalscorer in the league with his 151st Premiership strike in a 3–2 defeat by West Ham. He reached the 200 goal mark overall for Arsenal in the same month, and became the first man to hit 20 goals in five successive Premiership seasons in March. And all without so much as cracking a smile – just a Gallic shrug, a hug with team-mates and back to the centre circle.

Name Thierry Daniel Henry
Nickname Terence, TH14, Titi
Born Les Ulis, France, August 17th 1977
Arsenal appearances 364
Arsenal goals 226
International appearances France, 91
International goals 39

— THE FUTURE IS BRIGHT —

Arsenal achieved another English record on March 14th 2007 when the biggest crowd ever for an FA Youth Cup game turned up at the Emirates Stadium. Arsenal ran out 1–0 victors over Manchester United in the first leg of the semi-final, with 38,187 spectators there to see Kieran Gibbs score the winner. That figure would have filled Highbury to the rafters, and is higher than the total capacity of White Hart Lane. In fact, 5,000 more people watched Arsenal's youth team than saw Spurs play at home in the UEFA Cup on the same night. The bumper crowd was all the more impressive as the Arsenal first team were also in action on the same evening, winning 1–0 at Aston Villa.

The only Arsenal first team player on the pitch at the Emirates was left back Armand Traore. The 17-year-old French lad had appeared at the Millennium Stadium in the 2–1 defeat by Chelsea in the Carling Cup final the previous month, as well as featuring in other senior matches.

— CELEBRITY WAGS —

A number of Arsenal players have had wives or girlfriends who are famous in their own right:

- Arsenal manager Billy Wright was married for many years to singer Jo Beverley, a member of the Beverley Sisters. The melodic trio were a popular act throughout the 1950s and 1960s and were the first UK female group to break into the US top 10.

- In the late 1990s Tony Adams was spotted going on a string of dates with Wonderbra model Caprice. "I quite enjoyed the celebrity life for a while," said Adams later, "but then I am the same person no matter who I am going out with." The relationship soon fizzled out, but Caprice obviously picked up a few tips from the Arsenal skipper as, in 2006, she captained the England's women football team at the Celebrity World Cup Soccer Six. The team reached the final before losing to Brazil.

- In 2002 Freddie Ljungberg had a brief relationship with Swedish singer Denise 'DeDe' Lopez. "We met through a mutual friend and he was really nice and relaxed," Denise later told the *News of the World*. "I could tell there was a spark." In the same interview, the singer dismissed long-standing rumours about the Swedish international's sexuality. "I've heard the rumours about him being gay but I can tell you Freddie is all man, 100 per cent," she revealed.

- Ashley Cole and Girls Aloud singer Cheryl Tweedy married in some style at Wrotham Park, just north of Barnet, on July 15th 2006, shortly before the defender left Arsenal for Chelsea. The glitzy wedding was paid for by *OK!* magazine, with whom the couple signed a £1m deal to publish pictures of the event. Later that year Cheryl was voted the Sexiest Footballer's Wife by the readers of *FHM* magazine. Lucky Ashley.

- She may not be well known in Britain but Tomas Rosicky's girlfriend, Radka Kocurova, is a former runner-up in the Miss Czech Republic beauty pageant.

— THE NORTH LONDON DERBY —

There were many matches played between Arsenal and Tottenham Hotspur in the early years of the club, but it wasn't until the 1913/14 season that the Gunners became a north London club.

In the first meeting between the two sides at Highbury, on January 22nd 1921, Arsenal won 3–2 with Jock Rutherford and Henry White scoring the Gunners' goals in front of 60,600 spectators. Spurs, of course, had been furious two years earlier when the Football League decided that they should be relegated in the first season after the First World War, while Arsenal – only fifth in the old Second Division – were elected to take their place (see *Arsenal Up, Tottenham Down*, page 54).

Arsenal had to wait until the 1934/35 season before recording their first league double over Tottenham. The Gunners won 5–1 at Highbury, Ted Drake hitting the first derby hat-trick, and then trounced Spurs 6–0 at White Hart Lane. Arsenal won the league that season, while poor Tottenham were relegated after finishing rock bottom.

In 1949 Arsenal won the first cup game between the sides, Ian McPherson, Don Roper, and Doug Lishman all scoring as the Gunners beat Second Division Tottenham 3–0 at Highbury in the FA Cup third round. The first two-legged north London derby was the 1968/69 League Cup semi-final, in which the Gunners were again victorious. Two goals from striker John Radford saw Arsenal through 2–1 on aggregate.

More recently, the first non-British Isles player to score in a north London Derby was Dennis Bergkamp. The Dutchman was on target as Arsenal beat Spurs 2–1 at White Hart Lane during the 1995/96 season.

Overall, Arsenal have had the better of the encounters in the history of this fixture, winning 65 matches against their rivals compared to 49 wins for Tottenham. The full record between the two teams in north London derbies reads as follows:

	Arsenal wins	Draws	Spurs wins	Arsenal goals	Spurs goals
League	57	37	45	208	186
FA Cup	3	0	2	7	5
League Cup	5	2	2	13	9
Charity Shield	0	1	0	0	0
TOTAL	65	40	49	228	200

— MEN OF THE DECADE —

When the Premier League reached its 10-year anniversary in 2002, it brought together a panel of experts to decide who had been the best players during its inaugural decade. There were several Arsenal players included among the nominations, with David Seaman standing out statistically as the top flight's best goalkeeper, having kept the most clean sheets between 1992 and 2002. He was selected in the Domestic Team of the Decade line-up along with team-mate Tony Adams:

David Seaman

Gary Neville   **Tony Adams**   Steve Bruce   Stuart Pearce

David Beckham   Paul Ince   Paul Scholes   Ryan Giggs

Michael Owen   Alan Shearer

Meanwhile, the Overseas Team of the Decade included four Gunners:

Peter Schmeichel

Dan Petrescu   Jaap Stam   Marcel Desailly   Denis Irwin

Freddie Ljungberg   **Patrick Vieira**   Roy Keane   **Robert Pires**

Thierry Henry   Eric Cantona

Finally, the overall Team of the Decade included Arsenal's last two title-winning captains:

Peter Schmeichel

Gary Neville   **Tony Adams**   Marcel Desailly   Denis Irwin

David Beckham   **Patrick Vieira**   Paul Scholes   Ryan Giggs

Eric Cantona   Alan Shearer

— GUNNERS LEGENDS: TED DRAKE —

The amazing Ted Drake

Ted Drake was such a great Arsenal goalscorer that he still holds some records that even Ian Wright and Thierry Henry never managed to break. The athletic centre forward was also a keen cricketer and played for Hampshire, before settling on football as a career.

Drake's finishing ability led Arsenal manager George Allison to pay Southampton £6,500 for him in March 1934 – and he didn't let him down. In his first full season he smashed in 42 goals in 41 league games as Arsenal marched to the title – making him the leading scorer in Europe. Drake scored a total of 44 Arsenal goals in that 1934/35 season, which remains a club record. He slotted home on his debut for the club, as he had for the Saints, and also popped one in for England as they beat World Cup holders Italy 3–2 at Highbury in November 1934 (see *The Battle of Highbury*, page 35).

The striker was top scorer at Arsenal for five seasons, and was only 27 when the Second World War began, so it's reasonable to assume that his overall tally could have been much higher. He eventually notched up 139 goals in 184 games for Arsenal, and currently stands joint fifth among the club's top scorers of all time. However, his strike rate of around three goals in every four games is better than any other of the leading marksmen.

Incredibly, seven of Drake's goals came in one game against Aston Villa at Villa Park December 14th 1935, Arsenal romping home 7–1. His dribbling, control and finishing were at their peak on this day, as 70,000 fans packed into the stadium in Birmingham to watch the masterclass. Drake's seven-goal haul remains an English top flight record more than 70 years later. Drake grabbed the winner in the FA Cup final against Sheffield United later that same season, and won the league with Arsenal again in 1937/38.

He served in the Royal Air Force during the Second World War, before retiring from football through injury in 1945. He later became manager of Chelsea, taking the west Londoners to their first league title in 1954/55 and becoming the first man to win the League Championship as both a player and a manager – yet another record in the career of an outstanding sportsman.

Name Edward Joseph Drake
Born Southampton, August 16th 1912
Died May 30th 1995
Arsenal appearances 184
Arsenal goals 139
International appearances England, 5
International goals 6

— LIGHTS, CAMERA . . . ARSENAL—

Sabotage (1936)
Arsenal get a mention in the dialogue of this Alfred Hitchcock film.

The Arsenal Stadium Mystery (1939)
Gunners manager George Allison had a fairly big role in this thriller about footballer Jack Dyce, who dies on the pitch at Highbury while playing for a team called 'The Trojans'. Allison gives his famous team talk at half-time, saying: "It's 1–0 to the Arsenal. That's the way we like it". The match that the filmmakers shot in reality was Arsenal's 2–0 win over Brentford in 1938, during which the west London team wore white shirts so they'd show up better in the black and white footage.

Frenzy (1972)
In this Hitchcock classic the main character works in a pub that has a stained-glass depiction of Arsenal's 1970/71 Double triumph.

Rising Damp (1980)
Rigsby's local pub shows off an Arsenal rosette and scarf behind the bar, in this feature-length production of the TV sitcom.

Corrupt (1983)
Real-life Gunners fan John Lydon – formerly Johnny Rotten of the Sex Pistols – is seen carrying an Arsenal bag in this film featuring Harvey Keitel.

Lamb (1985)
Liam Neeson plays an Irish priest who ends up on the North Bank, after helping a young epileptic boy escape to London to watch David O'Leary play for Arsenal.

The Young Americans (1993)
Harvey Keitel is back in this gangster film that has scenes of Arsenal playing at Highbury.

When Saturday Comes (1996)
Arsenal are the opposition for a Sheffield United team that has wannabe footballer Sean Bean on the bench at Bramall Lane.

Fever Pitch (1997)
Arsenal FC is the star of this film about a boy who grows up to become a Gunners obsessive. Colin Firth and Ruth Gemmell are the love-struck couple who negotiate their romance around

Arsenal's 1988/89 championship-winning season. (See *Arsenal Fever*, page 11)

The Full Monty (1997)
Six unemployed men in Sheffield decide to become male strippers, with part of their act based on Arsenal's well-rehearsed offside trap of the 1990s.

Plunkett And Macleane (1999)
Two characters called Dixon and Winterburn pop up in this flick starring Jonny Lee Miller and Robert Carlyle as 19th century highwaymen.

Coyote Ugly (2000)
In this hit movie about dancing girls in a bar, Joe Strummer's ode to Tony Adams features on the soundtrack in a scene set in a music shop.

Muggers (2000)
An Arsenal scarf appears in this movie made by a production company called Clock End Films.

The Baby Juice Express (2001)
Arsenal fan and *Lock Stock And Two Smoking Barrels* star Nick Moran created this film, which features David Seaman as 'Huge Gangster' and Ray Parlour as 'Vince'.

Ocean's 12 (2004)
Hollywood heavyweights George Clooney and Brad Pitt don Arsenal tracksuits to aid their escape in this crime caper sequel set across Europe. Pitt's security man David Lindsay has a cameo role as 'Arsenal Bus Driver' in the film.

— CLEAN SHEETS —

Gillespie Road to the north of the old stadium used to be home to a steam laundry, which is why fans referred to the northern terrace as the Laundry End for the first 50 years of Highbury's existence.

— THE HIGBURY-DOME —

The old home of the Gunners provided the venue for five other sports during its 93-year history:

Baseball
Matches for the First World War servicemen over from the US were played on Arsenal's ground.

Boxing
London's own Henry Cooper fought Muhammad Ali there in 1966. Ali won in six rounds.

Cricket
Denis Compton, Jack Young and Leslie Compton all had benefit matches at Highbury, between Middlesex and an Arsenal cricket team, between 1949 and 1955.

Hockey
England took on the USA in an international women's match in 1955.

Rugby
Australia paid a visit to Highbury to play England in a fundraiser for the famine in Russia during the autumn of 1921.

— TV GUNNERS —

Small screens stars who follow the Gunners:

Clive Anderson
Kathy Burke
Alan Davies
Ainsely Harriot
Jane Horrocks
Paul Kaye
Matt Lucas
Rory McGrath
Dermot O'Leary
Linda Robson
Bradley Walsh
Ruby Wax

— WENGER'S BLIND SPOT —

It has become a bit of a joke in football circles that Arsene Wenger often claims not to have seen the most controversial incident of a match. Here are a few quotes from the Arsenal boss which suggest he might be in need of a new pair of specs:

"I did not see the Campbell incident."
After Sol Campbell had been accused of kicking Manchester United's Eric Djemba Djemba during the Community Shield, August 2003

"I don't know about food throwing. I did not see if something was thrown – you'll have to ask someone else because I don't know."
After Arsenal players had allegedly thrown soup and pizza at Manchester United boss Alex Ferguson in the Old Trafford tunnel, October 2004

"I didn't see the incident that led to Bergkamp's dismissal but I thought he had sent the wrong man off."
Reacting to Dennis Bergkamp's red card against Sheffield United in the FA Cup, February 2005

Wenger's failure to spot these and other similar incidents once led then Wigan manager Paul Jewell to quip after a game against Arsenal, "I had a bit of an Arsene Wenger moment because I didn't see the incident."

— GOOD OLD ARSENAL —

The Arsenal anthem, written by chin-stroking wonder pundit Jimmy Hill, will be heard at many a Gunners' game. It is sung to the tune of 'Rule Britannia':

Good old Arsenal
We're proud to say that name
And while we sing this song
We'll win the game

— JOURNALISTS GET IT RIGHT SHOCK —

Arsenal winners of the Football Writers' Association Footballer of the Year award:

1950	Joe Mercer
1971	Frank McLintock
1998	Dennis Bergkamp
2003	Thierry Henry
2004	Thierry Henry

Arsenal winners of the Professional Footballers' Association Players' Player of the Year award:

1979	Liam Brady
1998	Dennis Bergkamp
2003	Thierry Henry
2004	Thierry Henry

Arsenal winners of the Professional Footballers' Association Players' Young Player of the Year award:

1987	Tony Adams
1989	Paul Merson
1999	Nicolas Anelka

Arsenal winners of the Professional Footballers' Association Merit award:

1976	George Eastham OBE
1982	Joe Mercer OBE
2002	Niall Quinn

Arsenal winners of the Professional Footballers' Association Fans' Player of the Year award:

2003	Thierry Henry
2004	Thierry Henry

— GUNNERS LEGENDS: CHARLIE GEORGE —

Charlie George wastes some time at the end of the 1971 FA Cup final

Charlie George was the long-haired darling of the North Bank, the boy who made it from being a fan on the terraces to playing as a striker for the team. It was his wonder goal against Liverpool in the 1971 FA Cup final that brought Arsenal their first Double victory, a triumph Charlie celebrated in typically flamboyant fashion by putting the cup on his head. In that moment he crowned himself the King of Highbury, and he remains a legendary figure at the club to this day.

As England were busy winning the World Cup in the summer of 1966, Charlie George was also fulfilling his greatest ambition – he signed for Arsenal. The Islington-born striker soon became known for his swagger and total confidence on the ball, the likes of which would not really be seen again at Highbury until the arrival of Ian Wright in 1991. Glory soon came George's way as he featured in both legs of Arsenal's first European trophy success – the Fairs Cup victory over Anderlecht in 1970. But it was in the following season that 'the King' truly pulled the sword from the stone and achieved Arsenal immortality.

A broken leg wasn't an ideal start to the 1970/71 season for Charlie, but he was back in action for the title run-in and scored some vital goals as Arsenal and Leeds fought it out at the top of the league. With the FA Cup final against Liverpool coming up just days after the title was secured at White Hart Lane, the Double was on.

On a sunny day at Wembley that taxed the players' stamina, the game was goalless after 90 minutes. In extra-time, Liverpool took the lead but were soon pegged back when Eddie Kelly and George Graham between them scrambled the ball in for the equaliser. With just nine minutes left, centre-forward John Radford laid the ball off to a weary-looking Charlie who suddenly found the energy to let rip with a 20-yard shot that flew past Liverpool goalkeeper Ray Clemence into the net. Diving to the ground on his back, arms outstretched, the 20-year-old rebel and North Bank hero was mobbed by his overjoyed team-mates.

While George was a scorer of great goals, like that one at Wembley, by his own admission he wasn't as prolific as he'd have liked. But what set him apart from arguably any other player to pull on an Arsenal was his special relationship with the fans. He remembers: "I used to salute the supporters, because I had that repartee when I was on the terraces, then I came off the terraces and all my pals were still watching me. I like to think I played the game for the supporters – a little bit of a swagger, at times maybe a bit cocky, but then that's football."

Charlie eventually left Arsenal in 1975 – still only 24 – after one backroom row too many. He went on to score a hat-trick against Real Madrid for Derby County, and represent England. He played football in Hong Kong, as well as in Australia and USA, but Charlie always knew where home was. He is now back at Arsenal, working for the club as a 'Legend' matchday host, regaling fans with tales of his Highbury glory days in the 1960s and 1970s.

Name Frederick Charles George
Nickname King of Highbury
Born Islington, London, October 10th 1950
Arsenal appearances 157
Arsenal goals 49
International appearances England, 1

— BAD DAYS AT THE OFFICE —

The Gunners have had eight nasty humiliations in the cup competitions over the years, losing seven times to Third Division teams, and finally succumbing in 1992 to a Fourth Division team. January 1992 was a very happy new year for Wrexham, as they knocked English champions Arsenal out of the FA Cup while rock bottom of the lowest tier. It was very nearly much worse in 1956 as Bedford Town from the Southern League held Arsenal to a draw at Highbury, while as recently as 2005 Arsenal had a scare against lowly Doncaster Rovers, equalising right at the end of their cup tie to force a successful penalty shoot-out.

QPR 2–0 Arsenal
FA Cup, third round, 1921
Top division newcomers Arsenal faced Third Division QPR at Shepherd's Bush and were promptly dispatched from the FA Cup.

Walsall 2–0 Arsenal
FA Cup, third round, 1933
The Gunners were on their way to winning a second league title under Herbert Chapman, but were unbelievably sent packing from the cup at Fellow Park on January 14th 1933 by Third Division Walsall. Chapman was confident of victory and had picked his reserves to face the unfancied West Midlands team. However, the strategy backfired massively and Gilbert Alsop and Billy Shephard's goals won the match for the Saddlers. Chapman got rid of two of the reserve failures almost immediately, outraged that they'd lost to a Walsall team which had cost a mere £69 to assemble.

Arsenal 1–2 Norwich City
FA Cup, fourth round, 1953
Arsenal's first shock home defeat came in 1953 as Third Division Norwich won at Highbury thanks to two strikes in the second half. The result was all the more impressive as the Gunners again went on to be champions that season.

Arsenal 2–2 Bedford Town
FA Cup, third round, 1956
Plucky Bedford of the Southern League gave Gunners fans a few grey hairs in this match, the only time Arsenal have failed to beat a non-league team at home.

Northampton Town 3–1 Arsenal
FA Cup third round, 1958

Third Division Northampton caused a tremendous upset in 1958, sending the Gunners home from the County Ground humiliated.

Swindon Town 3–1 Arsenal
League Cup Final, 1969

Arsenal captain Frank McLintock was sure he'd get his hands on his first piece of silverware after this match, but his team somehow lost the cup to the Third Division team in the Wembley mud.

Arsenal 1–2 Walsall
League Cup, fourth round, 1983

The North London club's bogey team Walsall were back for more in 1983, as David slew Goliath again exactly 50 years on. This time, however, it was not the players who took the fall but the manager – Terry Neill was sacked after this defeat by the Third Division side.

York City 1–0 Arsenal
FA Cup, third round, 1985

Giant-killers York of the Third Division defeated mighty Arsenal at Bootham Crescent in 1985, with Keith Houchen scoring from the spot after Steve Williams had brought him down. Houchen went on to grab the winner in the FA Cup final two years later as Coventry City beat Spurs at Wembley.

Wrexham 2–1 Arsenal
FA Cup, third round, 1992

An almighty upset took place near the Welsh border as George Graham's champions were dumped out of the FA Cup by the team right at the other end of the Football League. Arsenal were leading 1–0 as usual until the 82nd minute, when veteran midfielder Mickey Thomas beat David Seaman with a free-kick. Moments later Steve Watkin hit the one of the most unlikely winners of all time past the England keeper.

Doncaster Rovers 2–2 Arsenal
League Cup, quarter-final, 2005

The South Yorkshire club from Division One were on course for an historic win at the Belle Vue Stadium, leading 2–1 with just minutes remaining. Then Gilberto Silva popped up with crucial second goal to spare Arsene Wenger's blushes, and Manuel Almunia was the hero in the resulting penalty shoot-out.

— THE SNARLING CUP FINAL —

The Gunners broke more records with their League Cup final appearance at Cardiff's Millennium Stadium on February 25th 2007.

Arsenal went into the 2006/07 final against Chelsea with nothing to lose. Arsene Wenger had played a combination of youth and reserve players in the tournament, and to his delight – and the nation's surprise – this makeshift team of youngsters had knocked out full-strength Everton, Liverpool and Spurs sides on route to the final.

The Gunners coach chose to stick with these young guns in the final rather than field his senior side against champions Chelsea, who had experienced world stars Andriy Shevchenko and Michael Ballack in their line-up. Arsenal's team included 17-year-olds Armand Traore and Theo Walcott, and with an average outfield age of just under 21, were the youngest side ever to play in a League Cup final.

After Walcott's goal made him the second youngest scorer ever in this fixture, it looked like Arsenal would pull off a shock win. But then Chelsea's top scorer Didier Drogba struck twice to win the Cup for the West Londoners, and the League Cup sponsored by Carling turning into the 'Snarling Cup Final'. Disappointed and frustrated, some of the Arsenal youngsters became involved in a mass brawl with the Chelsea players near the final whistle, resulting in a record three sendings-off – captain Kolo Toure and substitute Emmanuel Adebayor for Arsenal, and John Obi Mikel for Chelsea. Three previous League Cup finals had seen one player each shown the red card – but this was the first triple tunnel trudge.

Arsenal also hold the unwanted record of having fielded one of only two players to be sent off in the FA Cup final. Jose Antonio Reyes got his marching orders in the 0–0 draw with Manchester United in 2005, a game his team eventually won on penalties. United's own Kevin Moran was the first-ever player to be sent off in the Wembley showpiece, against Everton in 1985.

— GUNNERS LEGENDS: GEORGE GRAHAM —

George 'Stroller' Graham

George Graham is the only man to have won the league with Arsenal both as a player and a manager. As a cultured attacking midfielder, Graham was instrumental in the Bertie Mee team that won Arsenal's first European trophy and their first Double in the early 1970s. As a tough, disciplined coach he brought Arsenal's next two league titles, their second European win and three more cup victories.

Graham arrived from Chelsea in 1966, striker Tommy Baldwin moving in the opposite direction as part of the deal. He was Arsenal's top scorer for two seasons in the 1960s, before being moved into an offensive role behind the forwards. His all-round game was excellent, as an accomplished header, finisher and passer of the ball, but his lack of pace led to him being nicknamed 'Stroller'. In December 1972 he left Arsenal to captain Manchester United in a £125,000 transfer.

Encouraged by his old Chelsea mate Terry Venables to go into coaching, Graham had a successful stint as Millwall manager in the early 1980s. Noted by the Arsenal board for doing a lot with very little money, Graham was hired to take over from Don Howe in 1986. He soon replaced the stuttering first team with the wonder kids of the Arsenal youth system: Paul Merson, Tony Adams, David Rocastle and Michael Thomas among them. For less than £1m in total, Graham also brought in tough-tackling defenders Steve Bould, Lee Dixon and Nigel Winterburn to play alongside his new skipper, the 21-year-old Adams. Together, the quartet went on to become the most venerated back four in Arsenal history.

Quickly, Graham's youngsters developed a team spirit that belied their years, and the side's organisation and defensive strength brought success. The League Cup was won in 1987, and then in the 1988/89 season the league championship, after a dramatic title decider against Liverpool at Anfield.

Graham went on to sign some of Arsenal's most important players of the 1990s, such as Ian Wright and David Seaman. His side won the title again in 1990/91, suffering just a single defeat (to Chelsea) throughout the campaign. Graham secured the League Cup and FA Cup in 1993, and the following season lifted the European Cup Winners' Cup after a backs-to-the-wall 1–0 win over favourites Parma.

Despite these successes, Graham's team were increasingly criticised for playing defensive, boring, long-ball football. He was also responsible for some dud signings and a failure to find a suitable strike partner for the free-scoring Wright. Some of his players, too, had reservations about his regimented approach and nicknamed him 'Gaddafi', after the Libyan dictator. Graham's Arsenal reign finally ended in 1995, after he was accused of taking 'bungs' of £425,500 as part of the signings of Scandinavian players Pal Lydersen and John Jensen. The Arsenal board took a dim view of the allegations and forced Graham out. He was later found guilty of the charges and banned from football for a year. He returned to manage Leeds United and – somewhat incredibly – Spurs, before becoming a much respected TV pundit.

Name George Graham
Nickname Stroller, Gaddafi
Born Bargeddie, Scotland, November 30th 1944
Arsenal appearances 296
Arsenal goals 77
International appearances Scotland, 12
Arsenal manager 1986–95
Arsenal managerial honours League Championship (1988/89, 1991/92), FA Cup and League Cup Double (1993), League Cup (1987), European Cup Winners' Cup (1994)

— ARSENE'S CULTURAL LESSON —

Interviewed by former Chelsea manager Gianluca Vialli for his book *The Italian Job*, Arsene Wenger revealed the depths of his impressive intellect with a fascinating analysis of the differences between French, Italian and English culture and the effect of these differences on the countries' styles of football:

"If you think about it, the culture of a country is dictated by what they learn in school. We in France have Descartes. His rationalism is the basis for all French thought and culture. In Italy you have Machiavelli, who is also about being rational and calculating. Then in England, maybe because they are an island, they are more war-like, more passionate. They view football as an old style duel, a fight to the death, come what may. When an Englishman goes to war that's it, he either comes back triumphant or he comes back dead."

The passage had some English sports hacks scratching their heads. Who was this bloke Descartes? Didn't he play in midfield for France alongside Zidane? No, that was Deschamps. And Machiavelli? Surely, he meant Maldini, didn't he? In fact, clever old Arsene was referring to two important figures in philosophy: Frenchman Rene Descartes (1596–1650), who famously coined the maxim "I think, therefore I am"; and Italian Niccolo Machiavelli (1469–1527), after whom the word 'Machiavellian' was coined to describe the dark arts of political intrigue.

— ONE CAP WONDERS—

A list of the 13 Arsenal players who won one international cap each during their Gunners career:

Player	Country	Opposition	Year
John Coleman	England	Northern Ireland	1907
Alex Graham	Scotland	Northern Ireland	1921
John Butler	Scotland	Northern Ireland	1924
Alf Baker	England	Wales	1927
Herbie Roberts	England	Scotland	1931
Bernard Joy	England	Belgium	1936
Arthur Milton	England	Austria	1951
Jimmy Logie	Scotland	Northern Ireland	1952
Danny Clapton	England	Wales	1958
Jeff Blockley	England	Yugoslavia	1972
Jimmy Rimmer	England	Italy	1976
Alan Sunderland	England	Australia	1980
Brian Marwood	England	Saudi Arabia	1988

— WHERE THE HEART IS —

Tottenham Hotspur playing at home at Highbury? Arsenal playing at home at White Hart Lane? It sounds unthinkable, but it has happened. Spurs used Highbury for some games during the First World War, while Arsenal in return played home games at White Hart Lane during the Second World War years after their own stadium suffered bomb damage.

Here's a list of all the grounds that Arsenal have called home during their history:

1886	Plumstead Common
1887–88	Sportsman Ground, Plumstead
1888–90	Manor Ground, Plumstead
1890–93	Invicta Ground, Plumstead
1893–1913	Manor Ground, Plumstead
1913–2006	Arsenal Stadium, Highbury
1939–45	White Hart Lane, Tottenham
1998–99	Wembley Stadium (UEFA Champions League games only)
2006–	Emirates Stadium, Ashburton Grove

— LEAGUE CUP BOYCOTT —

Along with a number of other leading clubs, Arsenal boycotted the League Cup for a number of years after its inception in 1960. Believing that the new competition was an unwanted addition to an already crowded fixture list, the Gunners didn't enter the League Cup until the 1966/67 season when they were knocked out by West Ham in the third round. The change of heart was prompted by the award of a European place to the winners of the competition and by the fact that the original two-legged final was replaced by a one-off game at Wembley.

The following season, 1967/68, the Gunners reached the final of the League Cup for the first time, beating Coventry, Reading, Blackburn, Burnley and Huddersfield on the way to Wembley, where they lost 1–0 to Leeds in a dour match.

— MORE EMIRATES STATS —

Some of the fixtures and fittings at Arsenal's stadium:

4,500 metal handrails
More than 2,000 doors
100 stair flights, 13 lifts, five escalators
12,000 light fittings
Two cast iron cannons
4,500 IT/data points
41 TV camera positions
900 toilets, 370m of urinals, 113 disabled facilities
475 plasma screens
439 high definition screens
104 full-height turnstiles, 28 half-height and 13 glazed gates
– these can get 600 people into the stadium every minute
450 cash registers
16 trees around the podium
196 lightbulbs of 2,000 watts each
Two giant screens
56 roof speakers
Two sprinkler tanks, holding 400,000 litres in total
130 CCTV cameras
Four 8m x 6m Arsenal crests.

— ROCKY! ROCKY! —

David Rocastle has a strong claim to being Arsenal's most popular-ever player. The talented England midfielder rose through the ranks at Highbury in the 1980s to become one of the most exciting players of his age.

Within a year of his first-team debut he was voted Arsenal's Player of the Year in 1985/86. Rocky had an armoury of tricks up his sleeve on the wing, but could also play in central midfield where his strength, passing and work rate made him an influential figure. He won the League Cup with Arsenal in 1987, having got the Gunners to Wembley by scoring the winner against Spurs in the semi-final. He went on to enjoy further success with the club, picking up two League Championship medals in 1988/89 and 1990/91.

Although he was sold by George Graham to Leeds United for £2m in 1992, he was never forgotten at Highbury. Fans continued to sing his 'Rocky' chant in the stands, a tradition that continued after Rocastle died of cancer in 2001, aged just 33. Today his name is still sung at the Emirates Stadium, more than 15 years after he last played for the club – a testament to one of the warmest characters ever to wear the red and white.

Highbury celebrated David Rocastle Day in April 2006, just before the stadium's demolition, when Rocky's wife and children visited the ground for the 5–0 win over Aston Villa. The David Rocastle Trust was also Arsenal's charity of the season during the club's final year at Highbury, with funds raised going to the Trust's beneficiaries, Great Ormond Street Hospital and Cancer Research UK.

— REWARDING THE LEGENDS —

The Gunners have a long history of offering testimonials to long-serving players. The first such game at Highbury was a fund-raiser for the widow of Gunners star Bob Benson, who'd tragically died after playing a match in 1916. More recently, Tony Adams and David O'Leary were both awarded two testimonials by Arsenal, while Dennis Bergkamp's testimonial was the first match to be played at the club's new Emirates Stadium.

The Gunners have also hosted arch-rivals Spurs four times in testimonials – and lost on every occasion. Below is the full list of testimonials provided by Arsenal:

Player	Date	Score
Bob Benson	May 6th 1916	Arsenal 2 Rest of London 2
Jack Kelsey	May 20th 1963	Arsenal 2 Rangers 2
George Armstrong	March 12th 1974	Arsenal 1 Barcelona 3
Peter Storey	December 9th 1975	Arsenal 2 Feyenoord 1
Peter Simpson	October 9th 1976	Arsenal 1 Tottenham Hotspur 2
John Radford	May 10th 1977	Arsenal 5 Hajduk Split 0
Pat Rice	November 22nd 1977	Arsenal 1 Tottenham Hotspur 3
Ted Drake	September 11th 1979	Arsenal 2 Fulham 0
Sammy Nelson	September 25th 1980	Arsenal 0 Celtic 0
Pat Jennings	May 8th 1985	Arsenal 2 Tottenham Hotspur 3
David O'Leary	August 5th 1986	Arsenal 0 Celtic 2
Graham Rix	October 13th 1990	Arsenal 2 Tottenham Hotspur 5
Ray Kennedy	April 27th 1991	Arsenal 1 Liverpool 3
Paul Davis	July 30th 1991	Arsenal 2 Celtic 2
David O'Leary	May 17th 1994	Arsenal 4 Manchester United 4
Tony Adams	August 13th 1994	Arsenal 1 Crystal Palace 3
Alan Smith	November 10th 1995	Arsenal 2 Sampdoria 0

Paul Merson	May 8th 1996	Arsenal 8
		International XI 5
Nigel Winterburn	May 13th 1997	Arsenal 3
		Rangers 3
Lee Dixon	November 8th 1999	Arsenal 3
		Real Madrid 1
David Seaman	May 22nd 2001	Arsenal 0
		Barcelona 2
Tony Adams	May 13th 2002	Arsenal 1
		Celtic 1
Martin Keown	May 17th 2004	Arsenal 6
		England XI 0
Dennis Bergkamp	July 22nd 2006	Arsenal 2
		Ajax 1

— PLANET ARSENAL —

Arsenal had more players at the 2006 FIFA World Cup in Germany than any other club in the world (jointly with Chelsea). The Gunners contributed 16 players to the finals, beating AC Milan with 13, and Barcelona, Juventus and Manchester United on 12. Here's how a Gunners World Cup XI might have lined up:

1. Jens Lehmann   Germany
2. Emmanuel Eboue   Ivory Coast
3. Ashley Cole   England
4. Gilberto Silva   Brazil
5. Kolo Toure   Ivory Coast
6. Philippe Senderos   Switzerland
7. Cesc Fabregas   Spain
8. Emmanuel Adebayor   Togo
9. Thierry Henry   France
10. Robin van Persie   Holland
11. Tomas Rosicky   Czech Republic

Subs: Sol Campbell (England), Theo Walcott (England), Jose Antonio Reyes (Spain), Freddie Ljungberg (Sweden), Johan Djourou (Switzerland)

— TRANSFER RECORDS —

Arsenal were known as 'The Bank Of England Club' back in the 1920s and 1930s, but in recent decades their spending has been eclipsed by clubs such as Liverpool, Manchester United and Chelsea. Arsenal have still broken a lot of transfer records in their history, including twice holding the record for the world's most expensive signing (for David Jack and Bryn Jones).

Below is a full list of Arsenal's transfer milestones:

Player	Charlie Buchan
Year	1925
Signed from	Sunderland
Amount	£2,000
Milestone	Arsenal's first four-figure signing

Player	David Jack
Year	1928
Signed from	Bolton Wanderers
Amount	£10,890
Milestone	The first footballer in the world to be bought for five figures

Player	Bryn Jones
Year	1938
Signed from	Wolves
Amount	£14,000
Milestone	World's most expensive footballer

Player	Frank McLintock
Year	1964
Signed from	Leicester City
Amount	£80,000
Milestone	Britain's most expensive footballer

Player	Bob McNab
Year	1966
Signed from	Huddersfield Town
Amount	£50,000
Milestone	England's most expensive full-back

Player   Peter Marinello
Year   1969
Signed from Hibernian
Amount   £100,000
Milestone   Arsenal's first six-figure signing

Player   Alan Ball
Year   1971
Signed from Everton
Amount   £220,000
Milestone   England's most expensive footballer

Player   David Seaman
Year   1990
Signed from QPR
Amount   £1,300,000
Milestone   World's most expensive goalkeeper and Arsenal's first seven-figure signing

Player   Dennis Bergkamp
Year   1995
Signed from Internazionale
Amount   £7,500,000
Milestone   England's most expensive footballer

Player   Thierry Henry
Year   1999
Signed from Juventus
Amount   £10,500,000
Milestone   Arsenal's first eight-figure signing

Player   Theo Walcott
Year   2006
Signed from Southampton
Amount   £5,000,000 up to £12,000,000
Milestone   World's most expensive teenager

— TO CAP IT ALL —

Thierry Henry played more international games while with Arsenal than any other Gunners player. During his Gunners career, Titi picked up 80 caps for the French national team, scoring 39 goals. At the time of his signing for Barcelona in June 2007 he needed just two more goals to become Les Bleus' greatest-ever goalscorer, overtaking Michel Platini.

Henry's compatriot and friend Patrick Vieira is the second most capped Gunner, having appeared for France 79 times during his Highbury career. Both players won the World Cup with France in 1998 and the European Championship in 2000.

1980s Arsenal captain and left-back Kenny Sansom has the most England caps, with 77 – he scored one international goal, against Finland in 1984. He's followed by goalkeeper David 'Safe Hands' Seaman, who played for England 72 times during his career as Arsenal's No.1. Here's a list of Arsenal's all-time leading international appearance-makers:

Player	Caps while at Arsenal	Country
Thierry Henry	80	France
Patrick Vieira	79	France
Kenny Sansom	77	England
David Seaman	72	England
David O'Leary	68	Republic of Ireland
Tony Adams	66	England
Fredrik Ljungberg	60*	Sweden
Ashley Cole	51	England
Pat Rice	49	Northern Ireland
Sammy Nelson	48	Northern Ireland
Terry Neill	44	Northern Ireland
Sylvain Wiltord	44	France

Note: up until start of the 2007/08 season

— POLITICAL POWER —

Little were the Gunners to know at the time, but they had the future Finance Minister of Iceland playing for them at centre forward shortly after the end of the Second World War.

Albert Gudmundsson joined Arsenal in 1946, played as a striker for the North London club, and accompanied them on a tour of Brazil in 1951. He later played for a number of other clubs, including AC Milan.

After hanging up his boots, Gudmundsson worked in business before being put in charge of Iceland's Football Federation. In 1969 he helped set up a game between Arsenal and the Icelandic national team. He then entered politics, becoming Mayor of Reykjavik, and later the Icelandic Interior Minister and Finance Minister. He ended his working life as Iceland's Ambassador to France and Spain.

— ROYAL ARSENAL —

One notable figure to recently proclaim herself an Arsenal fan is none other than Britain's monarch, Her Majesty Queen Elizabeth II. The astonishing revelation made the front pages of the *Sun* in April 2007, after the Arsenal squad visited Buckingham Palace and the Queen declared her support for the club over more than 50 years.

The Gunners were invited to the Palace to make up for the Queen failing to attend the opening of the new Emirates Stadium at the beginning of the 2006/07 season – she'd been suffering from a back injury at the time. While chatting to the Arsenal squad, the Queen told the players that the Gunners were her favourite team.

"It seems the Queen follows football and she told us she was an Arsenal fan," Cesc Fabregas said later, adding proudly, "She appeared to definitely know who I was."

The Queen's Arsenal affiliations were also confirmed by a senior royal source. "Her Majesty has been fond of Arsenal for over 50 years," the unnamed spokesperson revealed. "Her late mother was a self-confessed Gooner, due to her admiration of their former player Denis Compton."

Meanwhile, the Queen's grandson Prince Harry has maintained the family connection by going to watch Arsenal at both Highbury and the Emirates Stadium.

— EURO SHUT-OUT—

Arsenal hold the current record for the most consecutive clean sheets in the Champions League. During the club's run to the 2006 Champions League final, the Gunners went ten games without conceding a goal – smashing the previous record of seven held by the 2004/05 AC Milan side.

The matches in which Arsenal's defence held firm included visits to Real Madrid, Juventus and Villarreal. Gunners keeper Jens Lehmann and his defenders also kept clean sheets in the home legs against the same teams, plus at home to Ajax, away to FC Thun and in both fixtures against Sparta Prague. The record-breaking run ended in the 76th minute of the Champions League final in Paris, when Samuel Eto'o equalised before his Barcelona side went on to win the trophy 2–1.

Jens Lehmann's sending-off in the final before the two goals were scored meant that it wasn't until the match at Hamburg in the following season's Champions League that he finally conceded a goal in the competition. The German keeper had gone 853 minutes unbeaten in Champions League games – that's 14 hours and 13 minutes. This is also a European best, beating Edwin van der Sar's record at Ajax in 1995/96. Lehmann took the crown from van der Sar during the semi-final second leg against Villarreal – a match in which he saved an 89th minute penalty by Juan Roman Riquelme.

— YOUTH v EXPERIENCE —

The oldest player ever to play for Arsenal was right-winger Jock 'The Flyer' Rutherford, who made his final appearance for the club aged 41 years and 159 days against Manchester City at Highbury on March 20th 1926. Title-chasing Arsenal won the game 1–0.

At the opposite end of the age scale, Cesc Fabregas is the youngest ever player to pull on the famous red and white shirt. The Spanish midfielder was just 16 years and 177 days old when he took to the field against Rotherham United in the League Cup on October 28th 2003.

— SOCCER STARS —

David Beckham is probably the most famous player from the English league to go to a 'soccer club' in North American, but Becks is by no means the only one to do so – numerous ex-Gunners have gone out to the USA or Canada in search of fortune, glory and the North American Dream.

Here is a selection of former Arsenal men to cross the pond to play in the North American Soccer League (NASL) or Major League Soccer (MLS):

Bill Harper	Fall River 1927–30
Joe Haverty	Chicago Spurs 1967
Brian Talbot	Toronto Metros 1971–72
Geoff Barnett	Minnesota Kicks 1976–80
Alan Ball	Vancouver Whitecaps 1978
Charlie George	Minnesota Kicks 1978
Peter Simpson	New England Teamen 1978–80
Alan Hudson	Seattle Sounders 1978–83
Peter Marinello	Phoenix Inferno 1980
Brian Kidd	Atlanta Chiefs, Fort Lauderdale Strikers, Minnesota Strikers 1981–84
Brian Hornsby	Edmonton Drillers 1983
Anders Limpar	Colorado Rapids 1999–2001
Steve Morrow	Dallas Burn 2002–04

— CAN WE PLAY HERE EVERY WEEK? —

The Gunners have scored more league goals at Villa Park than any other away ground. And while the Gunners have banged in 110 goals in 79 League games at Aston Villa's ground, the goals-per-game ratio is actually even better at Spurs and Leicester.

The five grounds where Arsenal have scored most league goals are:

Venue	Matches	Goals	Ratio
Villa Park	79	110	1.4 goals per game
Goodison Park	87	108	1.2 goals per game
White Hart Lane	71	108	1.5 goals per game
Filbert Street/ Walkers Stadium	58	92	1.6 goals per game
Stamford Bridge	71	91	1.3 goals per game

— GUNNERS LEGENDS: TONY ADAMS —

Tony Adams: Leader of men

The mainstay of the Arsenal defence for nearly two decades, Tony Adams is almost certainly the greatest captain the club has ever had. For England, too, he was probably his country's finest leader since the legendary Bobby Moore.

Adams started at Arsenal as a schoolboy in 1980, and stayed with the Gunners until his retirement in 2002 – after winning the Double for a second time. 'Mr Arsenal', as he was nicknamed, made his debut aged 17 against Sunderland in 1983, and within four years he had played for England, won the League Cup, and was voted PFA Young Player of the Year. At the start of the 1987/88 season he was appointed Arsenal club captain by George Graham, despite only being 21.

He led a sparkling generation of young Gunners talent – which included players such as Paul Merson, David Rocastle and Michael Thomas – that dramatically won Arsenal's first League Championship trophy for 18 years, thanks to Thomas's last-minute title-winner against Liverpool in 1989. Adams himself was at the heart of what became arguably the best back four in English football history, with Steve Bould alongside him in the centre, and Lee Dixon and Nigel Winterburn as full-backs. The quartet were instrumental in a second League Championship triumph in 1990/91, the Gunners losing just one game and conceding a mere 18 goals throughout the campaign.

Adams went on to captain Arsenal to two more title victories in 1997/98 and 2001/02, becoming the first English footballer to lead his side to championship success in three different decades. He also lifted the FA Cup three times (having headed the winner against Spurs in the 1993 FA Cup semi), the League Cup and the European Cup Winners' Cup.

Off the pitch, Adams underwent something of a transformation as the years passed. For much of his career, he had a reputation as a dressing-room prankster, an image reinforced when he accidentally dropped 1993 League Cup-winning goalscorer Steve Morrow in the post-match celebrations, breaking Morrow's collarbone. Adams was also known as an enthusiastic member of Arsenal's drinking club, and during the 1990/91 season he was jailed for two months after driving his car into a wall while over the alcohol limit. In 1996, shortly after performing heroically for England during the European Championships, he finally admitted to being an alcoholic and sought help for his addiction.

With new manager Arsene Wenger's help, Adams worked on recovering and reinventing himself. He wrote an acclaimed autobiography, *Addicted*, and set up the Sporting Chance clinic for sportspeople struggling with addictive tendencies. He began studying Sports Science at university, and took up playing the piano. The new, revitalised 'Tone' carried on at Arsenal until he was 35 – ignoring suitors Manchester United – and ended his career after 14 years as captain of London's most successful club.

Since leaving Arsenal he has managed Wycombe Wanderers and assisted Harry Redknapp at Portsmouth.

Name Tony Alexander Adams MBE
Nickname Big Tone, TA, Mr Arsenal, Rodders
Born Romford, October 10th 1966
Arsenal appearances 669
Arsenal goals 49
International appearances England, 66
International goals 5

— IF ONLY . . . —

The Champions League has so far eluded the Gunners, although it is possible to compile an Arsenal team of continental champions. Arsenal can lay claim to a full team of players who have won the Champions League or European Cup while with other clubs – and even have one in reserve.

Jimmy Rimmer (Manchester United, 1968, and Aston Villa, 1982)
Silvinho (Barcelona, 2006)
Gio van Bronckhorst (Barcelona, 2006)
Viv Anderson (Nottingham Forest, 1979)
Marc Overmars (Ajax, 1995)
Kanu (Ajax, 1995)
Davor Suker (Real Madrid, 1998)
Andy Cole (Manchester United, 1999)
Tony Woodcock (Nottingham Forest, 1979)
Nicolas Anelka (Real Madrid, 2000)
Ray Kennedy (Liverpool, 1977)

Sub: Brian Kidd (Manchester United, 1968)

— THE NEAR INVINCIBLES —

As every Arsenal fan surely knows, the Gunners went through the entire 2003/04 Premiership season unbeaten (see *The Invincibles*, page 4). Incredibly, the north Londoners came tantalisingly close to pulling off the same remarkable achievement more than a decade earlier, when they only lost one league match on the way to winning the old First Division in 1990/91.

Managed by George Graham, the Gunners' single slip up was against London rivals Chelsea, Arsenal going down 2–1 at Stamford Bridge on February 2nd 1991.

— IT'S AN HONOUR —

From three First World War heroes to the pace-setting achievements of the Arsenal Ladies in the 21st century, the British establishment has seen fit to honour Arsenal figures for almost 100 years now. High-achieving managers Bertie Mee and Arsene Wenger were both given honours by the Queen, as were famous players such as Denis Compton and Ian Wright. Here's the full list of Gunners to be awarded letters after their name:

Dr Leigh R Roose MM (Military Medal, 1916)
Dr James Paterson MC (Military Cross, WWI)
Charles Buchan MM (Military Medal, 1918)
Billy Milne DCM (Distinguished Conduct Medal, 1918)
Ernest North MM (Military Medal, WWI)
Ian McPherson DFC (Distinguished Flying Cross, 1944, and Bar, 1945)
Alf Fields BEM (British Empire Medal, 1945)
Tom Whittaker MBE (1945)
Denis Compton CBE (1958)
Billy Wright CBE (1959)
Bertie Mee OBE (1972)
Frank McLintock MBE (1972)
George Eastham OBE (1973)
Joe Mercer OBE (1976)
Pat Jennings MBE (1976) and OBE (1987)
Arfon Griffiths MBE (1977)
John Hollins MBE (1982)
David Seaman MBE (1997)
Tony Adams MBE (1999)
Alan Ball MBE (2000)
Ken Friar OBE (2000)
Viv Anderson MBE (2000)
Ian Wright MBE (2000)
Arsene Wenger OBE (2003)
Rachel Yankey MBE (2005)
Faye White MBE (2007)

— TROPHY HUNTERS —

The Gunners have enjoyed some of the finest moments in their history at White Hart Lane and Stamford Bridge, winning the title twice each at the homes of London rivals Tottenham Hotspur and Chelsea.

Arsenal clinched the league title at Spurs in 1971 and 2004, and at Chelsea in 1933 and 1934. Four other of the Gunners' triumphs came at Highbury, in 1931, 1938, 1953 and 1998. The club also picked up titles at Middlesbrough in 1935, Huddersfield Town in 1948, Liverpool in 1989, and Manchester United in 2002.

In a roundabout sort of way, Arsenal won the League at Nottingham Forest's City Ground in 1991, after Ian Woan's goal made Brian Clough's side 2–1 winners over Liverpool. The result confirmed Arsenal as champions, George Graham's team walking out to rapturous applause from the North Bank before dismantling Manchester United's defence in a 3–1 win – Alan Smith scoring a hat-trick.

Overall – of their 13 first-place finishes to date – the Gunners picked up eight titles in London, four up North, and one was settled in the Midlands.

— 12-GOAL THRILLER —

It's not often you get a first-class game in which both sides score six goals. In fact it's only ever happened twice, and the first time it involved Arsenal.

Leicester City went into half-time of their league match at Filbert Street against the Gunners on April 21st 1930 in confident mood, leading their visitors 3–1. But Herbert Chapman's team were not to be denied a result. The Gunners fought back, with stand-in striker David Halliday scoring four goals and Cliff Bastin netting twice to hit Leicester for six in total, while the Midlands team also got three more second-half goals to make it level after 90 minutes. The only time this absurd scoreline was ever repeated was when Middlesbrough visited Charlton in 1960.

— ARSENAL ALL-ROUNDERS —

The Gunners boast some of the finest ever cricketers to play professional football, in the Compton brothers and many others. The North London side has also fielded players who have displayed sporting prowess in other areas. Here are a few of them:

Alex Forbes	Wing half	1948–56	Ice hockey
Joe Hulme	Winger	1926–37	Billiards
Alf Kirchen	Winger	1935–43	Clay pigeon shooting
Alex Manninger	Goalkeeper	1997–2002	Skiing
John Mordue	Winger	1907–08	Fives (a game like squash)
Dr Kevin O'Flanagan	Winger	1945–49	Long jump, rugby union, sprint
Niall Quinn	Striker	1985–90	Gaelic football, hurling
Reginald Tricker	Inside forward	1927–29	Hurdles
Joe Wade	Full back	1945–54	Boxing

— ANNUS HORRIBILIS —

The Arsenal team of the 1912/13 season were so appalling, they have the unhappy distinction of having the joint worst ever First Division record.

A dismal three matches won out of the 38 played that year was matched only by the equally dire Stoke City side of 1984/85. However, Stoke played four more matches – giving them a higher chance of winning more games – and so statistically were the most rubbish team of the old First Division.

Arsenal's diabolical 1912/13 campaign also gave them the record of joint fewest home wins in a Football League season – with just one against West Brom six weeks from the end of the season. Sunderland, Rochdale, Blackpool, Notts County and Loughborough are the only other clubs to have had such a poor home season. Needless to say, the Gunners finished bottom of the League in 20th place, and were relegated.

— DOH! —

A selection of Arsenal players who have made some unlikely trips to the physio's table:

- Keen fisherman David Seaman managed to get a shoulder injury reeling in a 26lb carp.
- Perry Groves hit his head on the dugout while celebrating an Arsenal goal from the bench, and knocked himself out. Luckily physio Gary Lewin was on hand to assist the 'Ginger Genius'.
- Thierry Henry scored two against Chelsea at Highbury on May 6th 2000. When celebrating his second goal, Titi ran to the corner flag only to accidentally hit himself in the face with it, and have to go off in need of treatment.
- Patrick Vieira slid along the ground in joy after a goal against Manchester United, tearing a hamstring.
- David Seaman injured knee ligaments picking up his remote control.
- Charlie George chopped one of his toes off with a lawnmower.
- Most notoriously, Tony Adams picked up Steve Morrow after the Northern Irishman scored the winner in the 1993 League Cup final, but dropped him and broke his collarbone.

— CHAMPIONS TWICE IN ONE SEASON —

2004 was one of the best all-round years for Arsenal Football Club. For a start, the legendary 'Invincibles' season was completed, the Gunners winning the Premiership crown after an entirely unbeaten season. In addition, the Arsenal Ladies also won the league that year – hoisting up the trophy on the very same day that Patrick Vieira lifted the title.

Arsenal beat Leicester City 2–1 to cap off the glorious 2003/04 campaign, with the title already secured at White Hart Lane four games earlier. Meanwhile, success for the Ladies was less certain as they took to the field needing a win against Fulham on May 15th. But a 3–1 win for Arsenal's female first team meant a unique double league triumph had been achieved – Arsenal were the champions, twice.

— ARSENAL DO THE QUADRUPLE —

With a Smith goal in the 81st minute against Charlton Athletic in the FA Cup final on May 7th 2007, Arsenal secured a monumental achievement, becoming the first team ever to win the quadruple in one season. We are, of course, talking about the Arsenal Ladies – quite literally the greatest women's team the country has ever seen.

Before their 4–1 victory over Charlton in the FA Women's Cup final, Arsenal Ladies had already beaten Swedish team Umea 1–0 over two legs in the UEFA Women's Cup final. This meant that in their 20th season, the Ladies had become the first British team to succeed in this competition. A few days earlier the Gunners had claimed their fourth league title in a row with a 5–1 win over Chelsea. By this stage, the team had already overcome Leeds United 1–0 to win the FA Premier League cup and had, for good measure, outfought Millwall 2–0 to take the London County Cup home. The trophy-filled season was a triumph for Vic Akers, the manager, and his Arsenal Ladies team.

To acknowledge this record-breaking footballing year, the Ladies also received the highest honour Islington Council can bestow – the Freedom of the Borough. The squad and backroom staff all received a hand-written scroll, had their names put up in gold lettering in the town hall, and were offered free coffee for a year at a shop on Upper Street, N1.

"What they have done is truly remarkable, and we're very proud to have the best team in Europe right here in Islington," explained Islington Council's deputy leader, Terry Stacy. "We also want to acknowledge the fact that women's football is the fastest-growing sport in the UK."

— NOT ON THEIR WAY TO WEMBLEY —

According to Arsenal winger Perry 'The Ginger Genius' Groves, the Gunners' glory era of the late 1980s was inadvertently kick-started by the tannoy operator at White Hart Lane.

With the Gunners 2–0 down on aggregate at half-time in the 1987 League Cup semi-final at the Lane, new manager George Graham desperately needed a way to motivate his men. Then something amazing happened – something that got Arsenal's adrenaline flowing, and helped the team fight back to level the tie.

The Gunners went on to win the replay and the final against Liverpool, heralding the dawn of a successful new Arsenal age under George Graham. So what was the spur against Spurs?

"Tottenham's PA announcer did two things at half-time," Groves said. "He set out the ticket arrangements for the final, and they played the *Ossie's On His Way To Wembley* song.

"I was in the stands because I was injured, and while I thought the song was quite funny, it wound me up. God knows how the players felt when they heard.

"Someone went into the dressing room to tell them, and you don't need to give anyone more of an incentive than that – it would have added an extra yard to their efforts.

"At the time I thought it could come back to slap them in the face . . . and it did."

— A SPOT OF BOTHER —

One of the most bizarre incidents in the long history of Highbury took place in the old stadium's final season on October 22nd 2006. Leading 1–0 against Manchester City thanks to a Robert Pires penalty, Arsenal were awarded another spot-kick halfway through the second half. Once again, Pires stepped up to take the kick but, instead of shooting for goal, attempted to pass the ball square to the onrushing Thierry Henry.

However, Pires only managed to gently brush his foot against the ball, and got in the way of Henry as he raced into the penalty area. As the two players stood over the penalty spot, apparently unsure quite what to do next, a City defender forced his way between them and unceremoniously hacked the ball down the pitch. The home fans were left rubbing their eyes with disbelief, amazed that the two French stars had made such a mess of the simple task of taking a penalty.

Afterwards, a sheepish Henry was suitably contrite. "I take all the blame, it was my idea," he admitted. "If it had worked it would have been a brilliant idea, but it did not work. I want to apologise to Arsenal fans because maybe it was not the right thing to do."

Happily, the incident did not cost the Gunners dear, as they still won the match 1–0.

— 12–0 TO THE ARSENAL —

The Gunners have twice run up club record 12–0 wins. Ashford University were the first team to be hit for a dozen. The team from Kent met Woolwich Arsenal in the FA Cup's first qualifying round of the 1893/94 season, had 12 goals spanked into their net, and were promptly sent packing.

Seven years later Arsenal again thrashed the opposition 12–0, this time Loughborough Town being on the receiving end in a league game on March 12th 1900. The result was sweet revenge for Arsenal's biggest-ever defeat, an 8–0 league reverse away to the same opposition on December 12th 1896.

Arsenal's best away win was the 7–0 mauling of Standard Liege in the 1993 European Cup Winners' Cup, while the biggest home defeat for the club was a 6–0 thrashing by Derby County in the 1898/99 FA Cup campaign.

— YOUNG GUNS —

When Arsenal thrashed Blackburn Rovers 6–3 in the final of the FA Youth Cup in 2001, it was the sixth time the young Gunners had won the trophy. The club are second in the all-time list, with only Manchester United having won the competition more times – nine in total.

Arsenal's first success came in 1966, Sunderland being beaten 5–3 on aggregate. A young lad by the name of Pat Rice played in the tie.

To round off Arsenal's first Double-winning season in 1970/71 to perfection, the youth side also won their FA Cup, beating Cardiff 2–0. The squad's David Price later became an Arsenal first-team fixture, while Brendon Batson became Arsenal's first black player and had further success with Cambridge and West Brom.

The year before the senior's team next league title triumph in 1989 – culminating in the famous win at Anfield – Doncaster Rovers were dispatched by the young Arsenal team in a 6–1 win in 1988. The side contained future regulars David Hillier, Steve Morrow and Kevin Campbell.

Arsenal's first team won the European Cup Winners' Cup in the same year that the FA Youth Cup was lifted again, after a 5–3 win over Millwall in 1994. Midfielder Stephen Hughes went on from the youth ranks to the first XI.

And as Arsene Wenger brought new highs to the club after his arrival in the late 1990s, Arsenal won the FA Youth Cup again in 2000 and 2001. Arsenal's youngsters enjoyed a 5–1 aggregate victory against Coventry in 2000, regaining the trophy with the demolition of Blackburn 12 months later. Premiership players Steve Sidwell, Moritz Volz and Jeremie Aliadiere featured in the squad for the first final, and were joined by future top-flight stars Justin Hoyte and Jermaine Pennant in the second.

— SEMIS AT HIGHBURY —

FA Cup semi-finals have traditionally been played at neutral venues, and Highbury played host to 12 of them during its 93-year lifetime. These were the games watched by visiting fans in the North Bank (including those from Spurs who enjoyed a 3–0 win over Wolves in 1981 at their rivals' ground):

Year	Semi-finals teams and result	FA Cup final result
1929	Portsmouth 1–0 Aston Villa	Lost 2–0 to Bolton
1937	Preston North End 4–1 West Brom	Lost 3–1 to Sunderland
1939	Portsmouth 2–1 Huddersfield	Beat Wolves 4–1
1949	Leicester 3–1 Portsmouth	Lost 3–1 to Wolves
1958	Manchester United 5–3 Fulham (replay)	Lost 2–0 to Bolton
1978	Ipswich 3–1 West Brom	Beat Arsenal 1–0
1981	Spurs 3–0 Wolves (replay)	Beat Man City 3–2 (replay)
1982	QPR 1–0 West Brom	Lost 1–0 to Spurs (replay)
1983	Brighton 2–1 Sheffield Wednesday	Lost 4–0 to Man Utd (replay)
1984	Everton 1–0 Southampton (after extra time)	Beat Watford 2–0
1992	Liverpool 1–1 Portsmouth (Reds won replay)	Beat Sunderland 2–0
1997	Chelsea 3–0 Wimbledon	Beat Middlesbrough 2–0

— FIRST DIVISION BOOKENDS —

Arsenal's 73-year stay in the old First Division was the longest of any club. The Gunners were controversially 'promoted' in 1919 after having finished fifth in the Second Division, and were then never relegated – staying in the top flight until it was transformed into the Premier League in 1992.

The last match before Arsenal joined the old First Division was a 7–0 spanking of Nottingham Forest at Highbury, on April 24th 1915. Gunners forward Harry King scored four of his 26 goals that season during the game, while manager George Morrell bid farewell to Arsenal.

The first match after the First Division became the Premiership was a 4–2 defeat at home to Norwich City. Steve Bould and Kevin Campbell's goals weren't enough to see off the Canaries during the opening day fixture on August 15th 1992. The game was played in front of a limited crowd of 29,000 – plus a few imaginary fans, as Arsenal had just erected the infamous supporter-strewn mural to cover up the redevelopment of the North Bank into an all-seater terrace.

— PARACHUTE DISASTER —

Prior to the start of the 2007/08 season Aston Villa hadn't beaten Arsenal for nearly a decade. But what a strange, and sad, occasion the last time was.

Before the Villa Park fixture on December 13th 1998, the match ball was to be delivered to the referee by a skydiver – only for him to crash into the Trinity Road stand and land beside the players' tunnel.

Nigel Rogoff was a professional parachute instructor and competitor, but when the Villa Park stunt went wrong he was left with serious injuries and required 120 pints of blood to save his life. The match was postponed for 20 minutes as medical staff attended to the injured man, who was given a 50-50 chance of survival.

Luckily he pulled through, thanks to Birmingham medics and blood donated to the National Blood Service, but eventually he lost his left leg because of the accident.

Arsenal lost 3–2.

— ARSENAL 2 FRANCE 0 —

The Gunners achieved international success on February 14th 1989, taking on a French national team in a friendly at Highbury and beating them 2–0. The French side, including Eric Cantona and managed by Michel Platini, were beaten by goals from midfielder Martin Hayes and striker Alan Smith.

George Graham's players that day lined up as follows:

John Lukic

Lee Dixon   David O'Leary   Tony Adams   Nigel Winterburn

Martin Hayes Michael Thomas Kevin Richardson Brian Marwood

Paul Merson   Alan Smith

— MEAT AND FLOWERS —

The boardroom in the Grade II-listed East Stand at Highbury was itself a listed room. Clad in varnished oak, the boardroom was just above the dressing rooms, reached via the Marble Halls. Arsenal staff would decorate the room with flowers in the colours of the opposing team on matchdays, while on Sunday matches boardroom guests would be offered a choice of roast chicken or roast beef Sunday lunch.

The boardroom at the Emirates stadium, in contrast, isn't actually in the ground. It's in Highbury House, the Arsenal HQ building next to the stadium. The boardroom seats 15 guests for luxury meals at a large, oblong table on match-days – when a three-course buffet is served, along with champagne, wine and beer.

— DIVINE INTERVENTION —

Arsenal's crushing 6–2 defeat at home to Manchester United in a 1992 League Cup tie left many fans asking soul-searching questions. Prominent among them was to wonder if the thrashing meant there was no God.

Fortunately, none other than Britain's Chief Rabbi, Professor Sir Jonathan Sacks, was on hand to offer solace in this time of need. Having attended the game with a fellow Gooner – the then Archbishop of Canterbury, Dr George Carey – the Chief Rabbi explained: "What it proves is that God exists. It's just that He supports Manchester United."

— MR VERSATILITY —

Only one man in Arsenal's history, former miner Alf Baker, has played senior matches for the club in every position on the pitch. In 1919 Arsenal manager Leslie Knighton arrived at Baker's pit in Derbyshire, and beat the representatives of several other clubs to his signature.

'Doughy', as he was dubbed, was mainly used at right-half, but during his 12-year Gunners career played in all 11 positions – including several appearances as a goalkeeper. The most versatile footballer in the club's history was made club captain, represented England, and hung up his football boots on a high – having played for the first Arsenal side to win a trophy, the 1930 FA Cup.

— ARRIVALS LOUNGE —

The Gunners have introduced many nationalities to the Premiership. Here is a list of Arsenal players who were the first of their countrymen in an English Premier League squad:

Austria: Alex Manninger
Unused sub: September 13th 1997
Debut: January 31st 1998

Belarus: Alexander Hleb
Debut as sub: August 14th 2005

Denmark: John Jensen
Debut: August 15th 1992
(Peter Schmeichel made his Man Utd debut on the same day)

Japan: Junichi Inamoto
Unused sub: September 8th 2001
Debut (for Fulham): August 17th 2002

Liberia: Christopher Wreh
Unused sub: October 18th 1997
Debut as sub: November 1st 1997

Sweden: Anders Limpar
Debut: August 15th 1992
(Roland Nilsson made his Sheffield Wednesday debut on the same day)

Togo: Emmanuel Adebayor
Debut: January 13th 2006

— KANU CHAOS —

Nwankwo Kanu, the 6ft 5in Nigerian striker with the cult following, inadvertently added an extra fixture to the 1998/99 season by setting up an 'unfair' winning goal against Sheffield United in the FA Cup.

Arsenal were facing the Blades at Highbury in a fifth-round tie when the Yorkshire team kicked the ball out so one of their players could get treatment. The ball was thrown back in and received by Kanu, who hadn't realised the opponent had needed treatment, and promptly played Marc Overmars in to score what turned out to be the winning goal. Unsurprisingly, Sheffield United were furious.

Although Overmars' goal did not infringe any of the game's rules, football courtesy dictates that the ball is always passed back to the team in possession after a stoppage for injury. More aware of this tradition than some of his players, Arsene Wenger generously offered to re-play the match ten days later. The Blades' manager Steve Bruce accepted, the teams lined up again, and the Gunners triumphed 2–1 once more – this time without any controversy.

— VICTORY UNDER VICTORIA —

Arsenal won their first minor piece of silverware during the reign of Queen Victoria, when they held aloft the London Senior Cup in 1891.

The Gunners were an amateur outfit then, known as Royal Arsenal, and they beat St Bartholomew's Hospital 6–0 in the competition's final, held at the Kennington Oval. Having knocked out teams called Casuals and Clapton in previous rounds, a crowd of 6,000 looked on as the Woolwich club outclassed 'the Medicos' in the March 7th showpiece.

The team that was later driven home in "open carriages", accompanied by "shouting and singing" (according to the *Kentish Independent*), lined up as follows:

Bee

Connolly McBean

Howat Stewart Julian

Christmas Offer Barbour Gloak Fry

— GUNNERS LEGENDS: PATRICK VIEIRA —

'He comes from Senegal, he plays for Arsenal'

When Arsenal fans began wondering how on earth the club was going to find a captain to replace Tony Adams, along came Vieira. "He comes from Senegal, he plays for Arsenal . . . Vieira!", roared the North Bank to the tune of Dean Martin's 'Volare'.

The tall, tough French central midfielder gave Arsenal the grit in the middle of the park to match the effectiveness of its legendary 1990s back four. Opponents almost never passed him – they normally lost the ball to a long leg that came out of nowhere, hence Vieira's nickname, 'The Octopus'. His battles with Roy Keane – captain of arch-rivals Manchester United – were especially captivating, and Vieira often came off best.

In his nine-year Highbury career, during which he won three Premiership titles, Vieira was often judged to be the best midfielder of his type in the world. He was equally successful at international level, winning the World Cup and European Championships with

France and eventually becoming national team captain. For club and country his forte was linking defence and attack with quick, precise passes to close team-mates, such as Robert Pires, Dennis Bergkamp and Thierry Henry. Apart from his athletic aggression and forceful leadership, Vieira's trademark was his ability to create space in midfield, often confusing opposition players by flipping the ball over their heads as they came to tackle him.

Like his fellow countryman Thierry Henry, Vieira was another player rescued from an unhappy spell in Italian football by Arsene Wenger. He'd captained French side Cannes at 19, but went nowhere fast after a glamour move to AC Milan. Wenger picked Vieira up for a bargain £3m and he soon formed a formidable midfield partnership with Emmanuel Petit for club and country. The pair won the Double with Arsenal in 1997/98, before Vieira set up Petit for France's third goal against Brazil in that summer's World Cup Final.

Less positively, he was criticised for poor discipline at the start of his Arsenal career – in total, he was sent off nine times as a Gunners player. But on the pitch, Vieira just kept on winning. He grabbed a second Double with the side in 2001/02, two more FA Cups in 2003 and 2005, and took over from Tony Adams to skipper Arsenal through the entire 2003/04 season unbeaten.

His converted penalty to beat old enemies Manchested United in the 2005 FA Cup Final provided a glorious end to Vieira's Highbury career. Numerous bootleg reggae records about him appeared on sale around the ground, eulogising a modern-day folk hero, and in his last game at Highbury Pat smacked one in against Everton as the Gunners ran riot in a 7–0 win. Having flirted with the idea of joining Real Madrid in previous seasons, Vieira finally signed for Italian team Juventus, with Arsene Wenger satisfied that he was getting a valuable £13.75m for a player reaching the twilight of his footballing days.

"Patrick was a great player for us, one of the greatest in the club's history," the Gunners coach said. "I think his impact, not only at Arsenal but in English football overall, was just tremendous."

Name Patrick Donale Vieira
Nickname Paddy, *La Pieuvre* (The Octopus)
Born Dakar, Senegal, June 23rd 1976
Arsenal appearances 409
Arsenal goals 33
International appearances France, 101
International goals 6

— THE GUNS OF WAR —

With Highbury being used as an Air Raid Precautions centre during the Second World War, Arsenal played their 'home' fixtures during the conflict at White Hart Lane, the home of their arch rivals Tottenham Hotspur.

Gunners players during this era included such English footballing luminaries as Stanley Matthews and Stan Mortensen, both of whom made regular 'guest' appearances for the club. None of the matches that Arsenal played during the Second World War counted as official fixtures, but they still produced some fascinating feats.

The Arsenal game that produced the highest number of goals at Highbury came during the war – a 17-goal extravaganza. The home side beat Clapton Orient 15–2 in the qualifying round of the War Cup on February 8th 1941.

There were also two 12-goal games – an 8–4 victory over Charlton on October 21st 1939, just after war broke out, and a 9–3 mauling of Luton Town on December 2nd 1944, not too long before VE Day.

Here's Arsenal's full record during the Second World World War:

Season	League	Finish
1939/40	League South 'A' Division	1
1940/41	South Regional League	4
1941/42	London League	1
1942/43	Football League – South	1
1943/44	Football League – South	4
1944/45	Football League – South	8
1945/46	Football League – South	11

Season	Cup	Finish
1939/40	Football League War Cup	3rd round
1940/41	Football League War Cup	Runners-up (lost the final after a replay)
1941/42	London War Cup	4th in qualifying tournament
1942/43	London War Cup	Semi-final
1943/44	Football League War Cup	Winners
1944/45	Football League War Cup	4th in qualifying tournament
1945/46	Football League War Cup	Semi-final

And for good measure, this was how Arsenal got on during the First World War:

Season	League	Finish
1915/16	London Combination	3
1916/17	London Combination	5
1917/18	London Combination	5
1918/19	London Combination	2

— BUSBY BABES FAREWELL —

Sir Matt Busby's talented young Manchester United team of the late 1950s were tragically struck down by a plane crash in Munich on February 1st 1958. Five of the footballers who died that day – including captain and left-back Roger Byrne, striker Tommy Taylor, and half-backs Eddie Colman, Duncan Edwards and Mark Jones – had played their last match in England five days earlier in a 5–4 win over Arsenal at Highbury.

The game had been a marvellous example of attacking football at its best, with United going in 3–0 up at half-time, before the Gunners fought back in the second half to make it 3–3. United, whose team contained a young Bobby Charlton, bagged two more goals to go 5–3 up before Derek Tapscott scored Arsenal's fourth – but the Gunners failed to find an equaliser and the Busby Babes were triumphant.

It was a fitting finale in England for the careers of some of these players, whose lives were ended so young just days later.

— ADE'S BEST XI —

Arsenal's big Togo striker Emmanuel Adebayor took time out early in 2007 to pick his greatest ever world XI. And yes, it included fellow African striker Kanu:

Gianluigi Buffon

Lilian Thuram   Kolo Toure   Tony Adams   Roberto Carlos

Marc Overmars   Deco   Zinedine Zidane

Pele   Kanu   Diego Maradona

— WE'RE THE NORTH BANK —

Along with the likes of the Kop at Anfield and the Stretford End at Old Trafford, the North Bank at Highbury was one of football's best-known stands.

The stand went up in 1913 with the rest of the ground, was covered and refurbished in 1935, and then rebuilt again after it suffered a direct hit from the Luftwaffe during the Second World War. Traditionally, Arsenal's most die-hard supporters stood on the North Bank, a bounding and swaying mass of excited, singing North Londoners.

For 79 years Arsenal fans had been standing on the old North Bank, but in the summer of 1992 it was ripped down to be replaced by an all-seater stand. And its final game as an old-style terrace was to be a highly memorable one.

Arsenal's Ian Wright and Tottenham's Gary Lineker were locked in a neck-and-neck tussle at the top of the goalscorer charts as the 1991/92 season reached its conclusion. Wright lay in second place, with Lineker leading the race for that season's Golden Boot award by one goal.

In the Gunners' fixture at home to Southampton Wrighty got off to fine start with a penalty as Arsenal led the Saints 3–1, Kevin Campbell and Alan Smith netting the other two Arsenal goals. At this point, Wright needed just one more goal to become the First Division's undisputed top scorer in his first season at Highbury. Then, disaster struck – well, Gary Lineker did – in Tottenham's match at Old Trafford, leaving Ian Wright requiring a hat-trick to pip the Spurs star.

The tension built until the game reached injury time. Surely it couldn't go Wrighty's way now? But as the seconds ticked away, Satchmo yelled to keeper David Seaman to throw him the ball, collected it and skipped past two defenders, before unleashing a fierce strike low into the corner. The North Bank erupted.

The Saints kicked off, lost the ball and – as the ref thought about blowing his whistle – a cross flew into their box and Wrighty bundled the ball in to score. The goal, the last ever in front of the North Bank terrace, ensured that Wright won the Golden Boot with just about the last kick of the season. And gave the old North Bank the send-off it deserved.

— THREE IS THE MAGIC NUMBER —

Three Arsenal players have scored a record 12 hat-tricks for the club: Ted Drake, Jack Lambert and Jimmy Brain. Two of Drake's trebles actually came in the same game – the 7–1 destruction of Aston Villa in 1935.

In total the Gunners have notched 213 hat-tricks by 91 different players in senior competitions – Barbour and Scott being the first when they scored three each past Lyndhurst's keeper on October 5th 1889, and Julio Baptista being the most recent when he smashed in four against Liverpool at Anfield on January 9th 2007.

Here's the full list of all the players to score five or more hat-tricks for Arsenal:

Player	Hat-tricks
Ted Drake	12
Jack Lambert	12
Jimmy Brain	12
Ian Wright	11
Thierry Henry	9
Doug Lishman	8
David Herd	7
David Jack	7
John Radford	6
Joe Baker	5
Ronnie Rooke	5

— A MINER ADVANTAGE —

A selection of Gunners players who went from the pits to the pitch:

Name	Era	Position
Jimmy Brain	1923–31	Striker
Horace Cope	1926–33	Left-back
Wilf Copping	1934–39	Left-half
Samson Haden	1922–27	Winger
Jack Lambert	1926–33	Striker

— GUNNERS LEGENDS: BERTIE MEE —

Bertie Mee: Physio turned Double-winning gaffer

When Arsenal replaced manager Billy Wright with their physiotherapist Bertie Mee in June 1966, a few eyebrows were raised. Mee, though, proved an inspired choice as, assisted by top coaches Dave Sexton and Don Howe, he raised the Arsenal youth team to become senior champions, and brought the Double to Highbury.

After Mee's playing career was cut short by injury he trained as a physiotherapist in the army. When stalwart Arsenal physio Billy Milne departed in 1960, Mee was appointed as his replacement, but he quickly exuded a deep understanding of the game that went beyond treating injuries – which the Arsenal board were not slow to pick up on. Nevertheless, it was a surprise even to Mee when Arsenal chairman Denis Hill-Wood offered him the post of manager in 1966. He said afterwards: "My response was that if that's what the board would like, then I would give it a go."

With his military background, Mee brought his sense of discipline to bear on a skilful young Gunners squad. He assembled a balanced side that included the ultimately reliable Bob Wilson in goal, courageous skipper Frank McLintock in defence and elegant George Graham as playmaker. Up front, striking duo John Radford and Ray Kennedy formed a formidable partnership, supported by teenage maverick Charlie George who had the priceless ability to score a goal out of nothing. After years of mediocrity, Arsenal were finally on the march.

In 1968 Mee's side reached the League Cup final at Wembley, but lost 1–0 to Leeds United in a bad-tempered match. The following year the Gunners were beaten in the final again, this time a devastating 3–1 mauling in the mud by Third Division Swindon Town. This was a crucial moment in Mee's career. The team were down and out, and a disappointed Frank McLintock handed in a transfer request. However, Mee talked his skipper into staying and soon both their names were etched into the history books.

In 1970, Mee became the first Arsenal manager to succeed in Europe, as Arsenal defeated Anderlecht 4–3 on aggregate in the Inter-City Fairs Cup final. The following season, the Gunners were neck and neck with rivals Leeds in the league and also in contention for the FA Cup. As the elusive Double edged ever closer, Mee told his players in February 1971: "Now is the time for you to be really ambitious, and to aim for the success which may never be possible for you again in your lifetimes." The players responded by winning match after match to eventually claim the league and cup in the final week of an epic season.

Mee led Arsenal to another FA Cup final in 1972 and second place in the league in 1973, but the star of his Double-winners was fading. He left the club in 1976, becoming assistant to Graham Taylor at Watford. He was later made an OBE for services to his sport.

Name Bertram Mee OBE
Born Bullwell, Nottinghamshire, December 25th 1918
Died October 22nd 2001
Arsenal manager 1966–76
Arsenal honours European Fairs Cup (1969/70), League Championship and FA Cup Double (1970/71)

— GOLDEN GUNNERS —

Apart from his numerous other goalscoring achievements at Arsenal, Thierry Henry was the club's leading scorer in a record seven consecutive seasons. Ian Wright was leading scorer for six seasons, with Ted Drake and Doug Lishman both Arsenal's best marksmen for five. The three strikers who were Arsenal's most prolific players for four seasons running are Jimmy Brain, David Herd and Alan Smith.

Nobody has ever bettered Ted Drake's haul of 44 goals in the 1934/35 season. Jack Lambert had the highest tally before that, smashing in 39 goals during the 1930/31 campaign, matching the record of Jimmy Brain in 1925/26 and Henry in 2003/04.

Here is a list of Arsenal's top scorers, in all competitions, during each season since the club joined the Football League in 1893/94:

Season	Top scorer	Goals
1893/94	James Henderson	18
1894/95	Peter Mortimer	14
1895/96	Henry Boyd	13
1896/97	Patrick O'Brien	14
1897/98	Fergus Hunt	15
1898/99	Fergus Hunt	15
1899/1900	Ralph Gaudie	15
1900/01	Ralph Gaudie	8
1901/02	Tommy Biercliffe	11
1902/03	Tim Coleman	19
1903/04	Tommy Shanks	25
1904/05	Charlie Satterthwaite	11
1905/06	Tim Coleman	15
1906/07	Charlie Satterthwaite	19
1907/08	Peter Kyle	9
1908/09	Thomas Fitchie	10
1909/10	David Neave	5
1910/11	Jackie Chalmers	16
1911/12	Alf Common	17
1912/13	Charles Lewis	4
1913/14	Pat Flanagan	13
1914/15	Harry King	29
1919/20	Henry White	15
1920/21	Fred Pagnam	14

1921/22	Henry White	19
1922/23	Bob Turnbull	22
1923/24	Harry Woods	10
1924/25	Jimmy Brain	14
1925/26	Jimmy Brain	39
1926/27	Jimmy Brain	34
1927/28	Jimmy Brain	10
1928/29	David Jack	26
1929/30	Jack Lambert	23
1930/31	Jack Lambert	39
1931/32	Jack Lambert	27
1932/33	Cliff Bastin	33
1933/34	Cliff Bastin	15
1934/35	Ted Drake	44
1935/36	Ted Drake	28
1936/37	Ted Drake	27
1937/38	Ted Drake	18
1938/39	Ted Drake	16
1946/47	Reg Lewis	29
1947/48	Ronnie Rooke	34
1948/49	Reg Lewis	18
1949/50	Reg Lewis	24
1950/51	Doug Lishman	17
1951/52	Doug Lishman	30
1952/53	Doug Lishman	26
1953/54	Doug Lishman	20
1954/55	Doug Lishman	19
1955/56	Derek Tapscott	21
1956/57	Derek Tapscott	27
1957/58	David Herd	26
1958/59	David Herd	18
1959/60	David Herd	14
1960/61	David Herd	30
1961/62	Alan Skirton	21
1962/63	Joe Baker	31
1963/64	Geoff Strong	32
1964/65	Joe Baker	25
1965/66	Joe Baker	14
1966/67	George Graham	13
1967/68	George Graham	21

1968/69	John Radford	19
1969/70	John Radford	19
1970/71	Ray Kennedy	27
1971/72	Ray Kennedy	19
1972/73	John Radford	20
1973/74	Ray Kennedy	13
1974/75	Brian Kidd	23
1975/76	Brian Kidd	11
1976/77	Malcolm Macdonald	29
1977/78	Malcolm Macdonald	27
1978/79	Frank Stapleton	28
1979/80	Alan Sunderland	29
1980/81	Frank Stapleton	16
1981/82	Alan Sunderland	13
1982/83	Tony Woodcock	21
1983/84	Tony Woodcock	23
1984/85	Brian Talbot	13
1985/86	Charlie Nicholas	18
1986/87	Martin Hayes	24
1987/88	Alan Smith	16
1988/89	Alan Smith	25
1989/90	Alan Smith	13
1990/91	Alan Smith	27
1991/92	Ian Wright	26
1992/93	Ian Wright	30
1993/94	Ian Wright	35
1994/95	Ian Wright	30
1995/96	Ian Wright	22
1996/97	Ian Wright	30
1997/98	Dennis Bergkamp	22
1998/99	Nicolas Anelka	19
1999/2000	Thierry Henry	26
2000/01	Thierry Henry	22
2001/02	Thierry Henry	32
2002/03	Thierry Henry	32
2003/04	Thierry Henry	39
2004/05	Thierry Henry	30
2005/06	Thierry Henry	33
2006/07	Robin van Persie	13

— A CLUB IN MOURNING —

The whole family of Arsenal Football Club was devastated by the shocking early death of legendary manager Herbert Chapman. After he was lost to pneumonia aged 55 in January 1934, his assistant Joe Shaw stepped forward – with a poem he composed about Chapman – to help ease the suffering of the Yorkshireman's colleagues and friends.

This piece of writing is called *The Lost Captain*:

The Last Whistle has sounded, the great game is over,
O was ever a field left so silent as this;
The scene a bright hour since, how empty it is;
What desolate splendour the shadows now cover.
The captain has gone. The splendour was his.

He made no farewell, no sign has he given
That for him nevermore shall the big ball roll,
Nor the players he urged on, from his strong heart and soul,
Strive again with his skill, as they always have striven.
Not again will he hear when the crowd shouts: 'Goal!'

But somewhere . . . somewhere his spirit will quicken
With victors and vanquished. For now he has cast
In his lot with the Olympians of old who outlast
This human encounter, this football so stricken
That is seemed for a moment to die when he passed.

Who shall challenge his name, who shall challenge the laurel
We hold out to him through the twilight? His love
Was in beauty of action, and clean limbs that move
With the pride of high combat above the mean quarrel.
He led others to share it. And that is enough.

Not yet for those others the Full-Time is blowing.
The ball will roll on, they will cheer with their throats aflame;
They will think how this steel-minded man in his fame
Had dreamed while he worked, a dream ever glowing,
Of the glory of Greece in an English game.

— WHO ARE YA? —

Arsenal players with distinctive middle names include:

David **Reno** Bacuzzi
Gus **Cassius** Caesar
Sol **Jeremiah** Campbell
Alex **Rooney** Forbes
George **Melton** Grant
David **Bone Nightingale** Jack
Caesar **Augustus Llewelyn** Jenkins
Jimmy **Tullis** Logie
Archibald **Renwick** Macaulay
David **Carlyle** Rocastle
Charlie James **Fane** Preedy
George **Hedley** Swindin
Michael **Lauriston** Thomas
Chris **Anderson** Whyte
Bob **Primrose** Wilson

— SPORTING GUNNERS –

A team of sports personalities with red-and-white blood running through their veins:

Stuart Barnes, rugby player
Martin Brundle, racing car driver
Sir Henry Cooper, boxer
Frankie Dettori, jockey
Audley Harrison, boxer
Kelly Holmes, athlete
Jan Molby, footballer
Mark Ramprakash, cricketer
Daley Thompson, athlete
Michael Watson, boxer
Danny Williams, boxer
Frank Warren, boxing promoter (manager)

— ROMANCE OF THE CUP —

An outside-left of the 1910s, a certain Dr Jimmy Paterson, is possibly the only Arsenal player to have made forays down the wing while carrying a bunch of daffodils. A small girl handed them to him at the touchline before the start of a match, and it seems that Paterson didn't have the heart to throw them away.

— BANGING 'EM IN —

When your line-up includes the likes of Henry, Bergkamp, Pires, Ljungberg and Wiltord, all at the peak of their careers, then the chances are that you're going to bang in a few goals. Which is exactly what Arsenal did, starting in May 2001 and ending about a year and half later, by scoring in a record 55 consecutive Premiership matches.

Ashley Cole and Freddie Ljungberg began the incredible run, scoring against Southampton in a 3–2 away defeat on May 19th 2001. It wasn't until December 7th 2002 that this run ended, in a 2–0 defeat at Old Trafford. Along the way, the Gunners hammered the previous Premiership consecutive scoring record of 26 matches and, even more impressively, Arsene Wenger's side also beat the overall English record – that had been set by Chesterfield in 1930, when they managed to score in 47 games in a row in the Third Division (North).

By scoring in every game of the 2001/02 season, Arsenal set another record. Over the 55 games, 33 goals were scored by Thierry Henry, with another 54 coming from Bergkamp, Pires, Ljungberg and Wiltord between them.

— DODGY GUNNERS (ALLEGEDLY) —

A couple of supposed Arsenal fans you might not want to end up sitting next to at the Emirates:

'Mad' Frankie Fraser, ex-gangster
Osama Bin Laden, leader of Al-Qaeda

— GUNNERS ON THE AIR—

It might have something to do with being the biggest club in the British capital, but Arsenal have long led the way in broadcast innovations.

Highbury was the location for the first radio broadcast of a Football League game, Arsenal's 1–1 draw with Sheffield United going out over the airwaves on January 22nd 1927. The first goal that wireless listeners ever got to hear of live was scored by Gunners hero Charlie Buchan in that match. Arsenal were less fortunate with the first ever live FA Cup final broadcast that April, going down 1–0 to Cardiff at Wembley.

A decade later, a new technology called television arrived to cover football – kicking off, once again, at Highbury. The date was September 16th 1937, and the game was a friendly between the Arsenal first team and the reserves.

Nearly 20 years later, the first football match to be covered by ITV was Arsenal's 2–1 away victory over Bedford Town in an FA Cup third round replay on January 12th 1956. Meanwhile, a new football highlights programme called *Match of the Day* appeared on TV screens on August 22nd 1964, with the first game broadcast being Arsenal's 2–3 defeat to Liverpool at Anfield.

— RABBIT OUT OF A HAT-TRICK —

In the autumn of 1951 Arsenal striker Doug Lishman achieved the remarkable feat of scoring hat-tricks in three consecutive home games.

Lishman first popped up with three in a 4–3 victory over Fulham on October 27th. Two weeks later and the Gunners demolished West Brom 6–3, with half of Arsenal's goals notched by Lishman. A fortnight later Gunners fans were expecting more heroics from Lishman and they got them, as the striker bagged another three goals and the match ball in a 4–2 win over Bolton. No Arsenal player before or since has matched the inside left's prolific performances in those games.

— THE KETCHUP FINAL —

Apart from hosting numerous Arsenal games, Highbury also provided the venue for some less high profile matches over the years. These included the extraordinary contest between two sets of 14-year-olds in 2000, when Owen Price of Ernest Bevin College set a European record by scoring the fastest ever recorded goal . . . 4.07 seconds after kick-off.

Here is a selection of non-Arsenal matches played at Highbury:

October 26th 1938	England v Rest of Europe
May 3rd 1951	Metropolitan Police v Paris Police
April 30th 1952	British Olympic XI v England 'B' Trial XI
March 11th 1953	Floodlit Inter-City Football Match: London v Berlin
March 16th 1957	FA Amateur Cup semi-final: Wycombe Wanderers v Corinthian Casuals
March 27th 1957	British Army v Belgian Army
May 6th 1960	England v Young England
April 12th 1965	London Hilton Hotel v Regent Palace Hotel
May 17th 1999	Heinz Ketchup Cup Schools Final: Cardinal Newman RC v Kingsdown School
May 18th 2000	Heinz Ketchup Cup Schools Final: Barking Abbey v Ernest Bevin College

— THE HIGHBURY THRONE —

Two seats were often commandeered in the directors' box at Highbury in the 1970s for the visit of the King of Tonga. King Taufa'ahau Tupou IV was not a small man, and had to have two seats to accommodate his regal behind.

Arsenal chairman Peter Hill-Wood remembers the visits of the Tongan monarch to Highbury, as he "used to come regularly". His Majesty King Taufa'ahau weighed 26 stone, and had his position specially altered for him, with the armrest between two seats taken out.

— THE BEAST OF ANFIELD ROAD —

At the start of the 2006/07 season, Arsene Wenger signed on a year's loan a player he had coveted for some time – Real Madrid's Brazilian attacker Julio Baptista. Despite possessing an imposing build, Baptista took a while to adapt to the physical demands of English football. But, on a cold January night at Anfield in January 2007, he finally lived up to his reputation.

The occasion was a quarter-final tie in the League Cup, a competition used by both Arsenal and Liverpool to blood young players in senior matches. The two teams lined up with only three or four first-team regulars each, the referee blew his whistle and battle commenced. By the time the game was over, scenes that hadn't been witnessed on Merseyside for 77 years had been written into history.

The Gunners had won 6–3, humiliating Liverpool who hadn't conceded six goals at home since they were thrashed by 6–0 at Anfield by Sunderland on April 19th 1930. Another unwanted record for the hosts saw Julio Baptista become the first visiting player in 60 years to notch four in front of the Kop. Denis Westcott had been the last man to accomplish the feat, for Wolves in 1946. 'The Beast' also created a new Arsenal record – becoming the only Gunner ever to net four times in a League Cup match.

In the space of four days, Arsenal had knocked Liverpool out of both domestic cup competitions, having beaten a full-strength Liverpool 3–1 at Anfield in the FA Cup third round the previous Saturday. This 6–3 win was Arsenal's first League Cup victory at Anfield, and with it the Gunners became the first side to do the cup double over Liverpool. They also became the first team to beat Liverpool twice at Anfield in one season since Southampton did so in 1960. All in all, it wasn't a good night to be a scouser.

After the final whistle had gone at Anfield, and the Liverpool fans began to trudge home, the loudspeaker played the hit song 'Monster' by Welsh indie band The Automatic. The chorus went: "What's that coming over the hill, is it a monster?" It was, that night, and his name was Baptista.

— QUEEN VIC GUNNERS —

Although most of the characters in *EastEnders* proclaim varying levels of support for West Ham, many of the actors actually follow the Gunners. Here's a selection of Albert Square Gooners:

Actor	EastEnders character
James Alexandrou	Martin Fowler
Gary Beadle	Paul Trueman
Matt Di Angelo	Deano Wicks
Leonard Fenton	Dr Legg
Michelle Gayle	Hattie Tavernier
Mark Homer	Tony Hills
Martin Kemp	Steve Owen
Tamzin Outhwaite	Mel Owen
Patsy Palmer	Bianca Butcher
Joe Swash	Mickey Miller
Gillian Taylforth	Kathy Beale
Susan Tully	Michelle Fowler
Jessie Wallace	Kat Moon
Tom Watt	'Lofty' Holloway
Barbara Windsor	Peggy Mitchell

— SAME OLD ARSENAL, ALWAYS WINNING —

No other top-flight side has ever won as many games on the trot as Arsenal. The Gunners achieved this feat over two seasons in 2002 when they won 14 matches in a row, beginning with a 1–0 victory away to Everton on February 10th 2002.

The 13 straight wins Arsenal put together in the 2001/02 run-in is a record during a single season in the top flight. The previous best had been by the Tottenham 'Double' team of 1960/61, who had won 11 games running. Arsenal's victory over Birmingham City on August 18th, the opening fixture of the 2002/03 Premiership campaign, made it 14 wins in all – the run came to an end in the following game, a draw with West Ham at Upton Park. The previous best was also by Tottenham, 13 matches won in a row during 1959/60 and 1960/61.

Three other sides in English football history managed to win 14 consecutive matches – Manchester United (1904/05), Bristol City (1905/06) and Preston North End (1950/51) – but they were all in the old Second Division, so not as good.

— A DIFFERENT WORLD —

While today's players spend their time off covered in bling, hitting nightclubs and driving Aston Martins, the Arsenal side of yesteryear had slightly more worthy off-field pursuits. In a survey of Gunners from 1913, the players' pastimes included singing, foreign languages and chess. The manager George Morrell was into a spot of big game hunting, while George Hardy the trainer preferred shooting pigeons of the clay variety.

Notably, this squad contained an Adams, a Graham and a Groves, who partook in bowls, mathematics and whippet racing respectively. These are the hobbies the Arsenal squad of 1913 listed:

Player	Hobby
Adams	Bowls
Bell	Polo
Benson	Motorcycling
Burrell	Big game shooting
Caldwell	Badminton
Devine	Fives
Fidler	Aviation
Flanagan	Continental touring
Ford, G	Golf
Ford, W	Fencing
Graham	Mathematics
Grant	Skating
Greenaway	Lawn tennis
Groves	Whippet racing
Hardinge	Ping-pong
Jobey	Reading
King	Tobogganing
Lewis	Yachting
Lievesley	Shooting
Hardinge	Ping-pong
McEachrane	Chess
Peart	Curling
Randall	Sprinting
Rutherford	Boxing
Sands	Oratory
Shaw	Mountaineering
Stonley	Croquet

Thomson	Archery
Watson	Singing
Winship	Wrestling

— TEAM OF THE CENTURY —

According to official figures, Arsenal were the best team in England on average throughout the 20th century.

During the years 1900–1999, Arsenal had an average top-flight position of 8.5. That's better than any other team, including Liverpool who finished with an average position of 8.7, Everton with 10.6 and Manchester United with 10.9. Spurs came sixth in the century's league table, with an average end-of-season placing of 13.2.

Of the 89 league seasons played – 11 were cancelled due to the two World Wars – Arsenal were in the top division for 83 of them, and the second tier for six. And of those 83 seasons in the highest league in the land, the Gunners came top on 11 occasions.

The twentieth century top ten looks like this:

Position	Team	Average placing
1	Arsenal	8.5
2	Liverpool	8.7
3	Everton	10.6
4	Manchester United	10.9
5	Aston Villa	12.5
6	Tottenham Hotspur	13.2
7	Newcastle United	14.4
8	Manchester City	14.5
9	Chelsea	15.4
10	Sunderland	16.6

— THE DRAMA OF PENALTIES —

You might as well toss a coin, some argue, but in fact Arsenal have a slightly above average chance of winning the lottery of a penalty shoot-out, even though there's not much in it. In 14 matches that have gone to penalties, the Gunners have won eight and lost six.

The first of these was in the 1980 European Cup Winners' Cup final, the Gunners going down 5–4 on spot-kicks to Spanish side Valencia after a 0–0 draw. Arsenal have since played in two other finals to be settled by penalties: the 2000 UEFA Cup final, which the Gunners eventually lost to Turkish outfit Galatasaray; and the 2005 FA Cup final at the Millennium stadium in Cardiff when, after a disappointing display against Manchester United, the north Londoners collected the trophy thanks to Ashley Cole's spot-kick winner.

Here is the full list of Arsenal matches settled by penalties:

European Cup Winners' Cup final
May 14th 1980
Valencia 0–0 Arsenal
Penalties: Valencia 5–4 Arsenal

League Cup, second round, second leg
October 7th 1992
Millwall 1–1 Arsenal
Penalties: Millwall 1–3 Arsenal

FA Charity Shield
August 7th 1993
Manchester United 1–1 Arsenal
Penalties: Manchester United 5–4 Arsenal

European Cup Winners' Cup semi-final, second leg
April 20th 1995
Sampdoria 3–2 Arsenal (5–5 on aggregate)
Penalties: Sampdoria 2–3 Arsenal

FA Cup third round replay
January 14th 1998
Port Vale 1–1 Arsenal
Penalties: Port Vale 3–4 Arsenal

FA Cup quarter-final replay
March 17th 1998
West Ham 1–1 Arsenal
Penalties: West Ham 3–4 Arsenal

League Cup fourth round
November 30th 1999
Middlesbrough 2–2 Arsenal
Penalties: Middlesbrough 3–1 Arsenal

FA Cup fourth round replay
January 19th 2000
Leicester City 0–0 Arsenal
Penalties: Leicester City 6–5 Arsenal

UEFA Cup final
May 17th 2000
Galatasaray 0–0 Arsenal
Penalties: Galatasaray 4–1 Arsenal

FA Community Shield
August 10th 2003
Manchester United 1–1 Arsenal
Penalties: Manchester United 4–3 Arsenal

League Cup third round
October 28th 2003
Arsenal 1–1 Rotherham
Penalties: Arsenal 9–8 Rotherham

FA Cup fifth round replay
March 1st 2005
Sheffield United 0–0 Arsenal
Penalties: Sheffield United 2–4 Arsenal

FA Cup final
May 18th 2005
Arsenal 0–0 Manchester United
Penalties: Arsenal 5–4 Manchester United

League Cup quarter-final
December 21st 2005
Doncaster Rovers 2–2 Arsenal
Penalties: Doncaster Rovers 1–3 Arsenal

— CAN WE PLAY YOU EVERY WEEK? —

Arsenal hold the record for the most consecutive victories against another Premiership club, with 11 against Manchester City.

The miserable sequence for City began in August 1994, and didn't end until January 4th 2005, when they finally managed a 1–1 draw at Highbury. Arsenal scored 30 goals in the 11-game run, conceding six – and never more than one in a game. Here's the full list of record-breaking results:

Season	Date	Venue	Result
1994/95	August 20th 1994	Highbury	Arsenal won 3–0
1994/95	December 12th 1994	Maine Road	Arsenal won 2–1
1995/96	September 10th 1995	Maine Road	Arsenal won 1–0
1995/96	March 5th 1996	Highbury	Arsenal won 3–1
2000/01	October 28th 2000	Highbury	Arsenal won 5–0
2000/01	April 11th 2001	Maine Road	Arsenal won 4–0
2002/03	September 10th 2002	Highbury	Arsenal won 2–1
2002/03	February 22nd 2003	Maine Road	Arsenal won 5–1
2003/04	August 31st 2003	City of Manchester	Arsenal won 2–1
2003/04	February 1st 2004	Highbury	Arsenal won 2–1
2004/05	September 25th 2004	City of Manchester	Arsenal won 1–0

— RED AND WHITE VINYL —

Inspired by their favourite terrace anthems or chants, a number of Gooners have recorded tracks about the team. While some of these songs have been put together by groups of die-hard fans, a handful of big-time music names such as Joe Strummer and Half Man Half Biscuit have also recorded songs about Arsenal players. Here's a list of some of the Gunners-related songs that made it on to vinyl, cassette, CD or MP3:

'I Wish I Could Play Like Charlie George' – The Strikers and Selston Bagthorpe Primary School Choir (1972)
'Dial Square' – Midway Still (1992)
'The Victory Song' – Enrico Cocozza (1993)
'Highbury Heartbeat' – The IASA Wembley Mix (1993)
'Arriverderci Liam' – Stephen North and the Flat Back Four (1995)

'The Gus Caesar Rap' – Stephen North and the Flat Back Four (1995)

'The Charlie George Calypso' – Stephen North and the Flat Back Four (1995)

'Arsenal Rap' – The A Team (1995)

'Gooneroonie' – The A Team (1995)

'Come On You Gunners' – Tina and the North Bank (1995)

'Ooh Ooh Tony Adams' – The A Team (1995)

'Come On You Reds' –The Arsenal Supporters (1995)

'One Night At Anfield' – Top Gooner (1995)

'The Only Cockney Rebel (That Meant Anything To Me Was Charlie George)' – The Half Time Oranges (1998)

'Tony Adams' – Joe Strummer and the Mescaleros (1999)

'Bob Wilson: Anchor Man' – Half Man Half Biscuit (2001)

'Vieira' – Jackin' The Box and DJ Fresh (2001)

'We Are Arsenal' – Wenger Boys (2001)

'Highbury Sunshine' – Yeah (2001)

'Mr Bergkamp' – Yeah (2001)

'Thierry Henry Song' – The Away Crew' (2001)

'Thierry Henry' – Arsene Sings (2001)

'We All Follow The Arsenal' – The Away Crew (2001)

'Beautiful Goal' – Pick 'n' Mix (2002)

'A.R.S.E.N.A.L. Up The Gunners' – Arsenal Choir (2002)

'Perry Groves World' – The Ginger Nuts (2002)

'Arsenal' – Tina and the North Bank (2002)

'Sol's A Gooner' – The Vieira Boys (2002)

— FIRST 'FOREIGN' VISITORS —

Highbury holds the distinction of being the first ground to act as venue for an England international against a team not from the home nations. The national side of Belgium arrived in north London on March 19th 1923 for the historic international match, and were promptly dispatched 6–1.

Only 14,052 turned up to see the England victory in the friendly match, in which the home team's goals were scored by Kenneth Hegan (two), Harry Chambers, David Mercer, Jimmy Seed and Norman Bullock.

Highbury had already hosted one England game before that, against Wales in March 1920. Wales won 2–1 that day, England's only defeat in 13 internationals at Highbury.

— CHIN UP —

One of the strangest incidents at Highbury occurred during a match between Arsenal and Liverpool in September 1972. Dennis Drewitt was one of the linesmen for that fixture, but pulled a muscle during the game and couldn't carry on running the line. In those days there was no designated fourth official and with no available replacement the game was in danger of being called off.

In desperation, the stadium announcer asked if there was a qualified referee in the ground who could step in. And sure enough, a man presented himself. A man with a referee's certificate and an usually large chin. It was football pundit Jimmy Hill.

Jimmy was given a tracksuit, and proceeded to work the line for the rest of the match, which finished 0–0. It was the second time the former Coventry boss had had an influence on Arsenal Football Club – the previous year he had written the words to the Gunners' FA Cup final song, *Good Old Arsenal*, to the tune of *Rule Britannia* (see *Good Old Arsenal*, page 82).

— WE ALL LIVE IN AN IAN WRIGHT HOUSE —

Ian Wright was undoubtedly a cult figure at Highbury. But even so, it's unlikely that the conversion of the stadium into flats will see a block named after him. It was a different story, though, when the Woolwich Building Society created a block of flats named 'Ian Wright' in Harlow, Essex. The firm also built three others called 'Kevin Campbell', 'Paul Davis' and – believe it or not – 'John Jensen', in homage to the Arsenal side that had just won the European Cup Winners' Cup in 1994.

As its name suggests, the Woolwich Building Society was founded just yards away from where the Arsenal Football Club was established, in Woolwich, south-east London, and decided to draw inspiration from their joint roots in their latest marketing initiative. However, after the firm decided that there were more Spurs than Arsenal fans in that area of Essex, the Campbell, Davis, Jensen and Wright buildings in the Church Langley estate were re-named before they were advertised in estate agents' windows.

— CAPITAL KINGS —

Under Arsene Wenger the Gunners managed to go almost three seasons without losing a domestic London derby. These triumphant years in the capital ran from November 2001 to the end of the 2003/04 season, and the 29 unbeaten results ran like this:

Season 2001/02	Opposition	Venue	Result
November 17th 2001	Spurs	Away draw	1–1
December 15th 2001	West Ham	Away draw	1–1
December 26th 2001	Chelsea	Home win	2–1
February 23rd 2002	Fulham	Home win	4–1
April 1st 2002	Charlton	Away win	3–0
April 6th 2002	Spurs	Home win	2–1
April 24th 2002	West Ham	Home win	2–0
May 4th 2002	Chelsea	FA Cup final, Cardiff, win	2–0
Season 2002/03			
24 August	West Ham	Home draw	2–2
1 September	Chelsea	Away draw	1–1
14 September	Charlton	Away win	3–0
3 November	Fulham	Away win	1–0
16 November	Spurs	Home win	3–0
15 December	Spurs	Away draw	1–1
1 January	Chelsea	Home win	3–2
19 January	West Ham	Home win	3–1
1 February	Fulham	Home win	2–1
2 March	Charlton	Home win	2–0
8 March	Chelsea	FA Cup 6th round, home draw	2–2
25 March	Chelsea	FA Cup 6th round replay, away win	3–1
Season 2003/04			
18 October	Chelsea	Home win	2–1
26 October	Charlton	Away draw	1–1
8 November	Spurs	Home win	2–1
30 November	Fulham	Home draw	0–0

15 February	Chelsea	FA Cup 5th round, home win	2–1
21 February	Chelsea	Away win	2–1
28 February	Charlton	Home win	2–1
25 April	Spurs	Away draw	1–1
9 May	Fulham	Away win	1–0

— BATS AND BALLS —

A great many Gunners players have also been top cricketers. Denis Compton stood out as the outstanding example, representing England at both football and cricket. But all these Arsenal footballers could also bat or bowl with the best of them:

Don Bennett	Middlesex
Brian Close	Yorkshire, Somerset and England
Denis Compton	Middlesex and England
Leslie Compton	Middlesex
George Cox	Sussex
Ted Drake	Hampshire
Andy Ducat	Surrey and England
Ian Gould	Middlesex and Sussex
Jimmy Gray	Hampshire
Wally Hardinge	Kent and England
Joe Hulme	Middlesex
Arthur Milton	Gloucestershire and England
Harry Murrell	Kent and Middlesex
Ernest North	Middlesex
Ralph Prouton	Hampshire
Don Roper	Hampshire
Jim Standen	Worcestershire
Ernest Stanley	Essex
Harry Storer	Derbyshire
Ray Swallow	Derbyshire
H.A. White	Warwickshire

— EMIRATES LEGENDS —

The seven former Arsenal greats on hand to take fans on a 'Legends Tour' of the Emirates Stadium in its inaugural season were:

- Paul Davis: League winner in 1989 and 1991
- Charlie George: Double winner in 1971
- Perry Groves: League winner in 1989
- Sammy Nelson: FA Cup winner in 1979
- John Radford: Double winner in 1971
- Kenny Sansom: League Cup winner in 1987
- Bob Wilson: Double winner in 1971

— M PEOPLE'S AFC PEOPLE —

Shovell, BBC radio presenter and drummer of the group M People, is a huge fan of the Gunners. His favourite ever player is Charlie George, though Charlie wouldn't make his all-time Arsenal XI. This is who Shovell would heap out on the turf:

David Seaman

Viv Anderson   Tony Adams   Martin Keown   Kenny Sansom

Marc Overmars   Liam Brady   Patrick Vieira   Paul Merson

Ian Wright   Dennis Bergkamp

— MISCELLANEOUS SEASONAL RECORDS —

Highest points total: 90, 2003/04
Most league wins: 28, 1930/31
Most home wins: 18, 1970/71
Most away wins: 14, 1930/31 and 2001/02
Fewest defeats: 0, 2003/04
Fewest home defeats: 0, on six occasions
Fewest away defeats: 0, 2001/02 and 2003/04

Lowest points total: 18, 1912/13
Fewest league wins: 3, 1912/13
Fewest home wins: 1, 1912/13
Fewest away wins: 2, 1900/01, 1912/13, 1924/25 and 1975/76
Most defeats: 23, 1912/13 and 1924/25
Most home defeats: 10, 1912/13
Most away defeats: 17, 1924/25

Most league goals scored: 127, 1930/31
Most goals scored at home: 74, 1934/35
Most goals scored away: 60, 1930/31
Fewest goals conceded: 17, 1998/99
Fewest goals conceded at home: 5, 1903/04 and 1998/99
Fewest goals conceded away: 8, 1990/91

Fewest league goals scored: 26, 1912/13
Fewest goals scored at home: 11, 1912/13
Fewest goals scored away: 9, 1900/01
Most goals conceded: 86, 1926/27 and 1927/28
Most goals conceded at home: 39, 1957/58
Most goals conceded away: 56, 1926/27

Most league draws: 18, 1969/70
Most home draws: 10, 1936/37, 1969/70 and 1979/80
Most away draws: 10, 1947/48
Fewest draws: 4, on five occasions
Fewest home draws: 1, on six occasions
Fewest away draws: 1, 1921/22

— ARSENAL'S SEASON BY SEASON RECORD —

Season	Div	P	Home					Away					Pts	GD	Pos
			W	D	L	F	A	W	D	L	F	A			
1893/94	(2)	28	9	1	4	33	19	3	3	8	19	36	28	-3	9th
1894/95	(2)	30	11	3	1	54	20	3	3	9	21	38	34	17	8th
1895/96	(2)	30	11	1	3	43	11	3	3	9	16	31	32	17	7th
1896/97	(2)	30	10	1	4	42	20	3	3	9	26	50	30	-2	10th
1897/98	(2)	30	10	4	1	41	14	6	1	8	28	35	37	20	5th
1898/99	(2)	34	14	2	1	55	10	4	3	10	17	31	41	31	7th
1899/00	(2)	34	13	1	3	47	12	3	3	11	14	31	36	18	8th
1900/01	(2)	34	13	3	1	30	11	2	3	12	9	24	36	4	7th
1901/02	(2)	34	13	2	2	35	9	5	4	8	15	17	42	24	4th
1902/03	(2)	34	14	2	1	46	9	6	6	5	20	21	48	36	3rd
1903/04	(2)	34	15	2	0	67	5	6	5	6	24	17	49	69	2nd(PR)
1904/05	(1)	34	9	5	3	19	12	3	4	10	17	28	33	-4	10th
1905/06	(1)	38	12	4	3	43	21	3	3	13	19	43	37	-2	12th
1906/07	(1)	38	15	1	3	38	15	5	3	11	28	44	44	7	7th
1907/08	(1)	38	9	8	2	32	18	3	4	12	19	45	36	-12	15th
1908/09	(1)	38	9	3	7	24	18	5	7	7	28	31	38	3	6th
1909/10	(1)	38	6	5	8	17	19	5	4	10	20	48	31	-30	18th
1910/11	(1)	38	9	6	4	24	14	4	6	9	17	35	38	-8	10th
1911/12	(1)	38	12	3	4	38	19	3	5	11	17	40	38	-4	10th
1912/13	(1)	38	1	8	10	11	31	2	4	13	15	43	18	-48	20th (R)
1913/14	(2)	38	14	3	2	34	10	6	6	7	20	28	49	16	3rd
1914/15	(2)	38	15	1	3	52	13	4	4	11	17	28	43	28	5th (PR)
WORLD WAR I															
1919/20	(1)	42	11	5	5	32	21	4	7	10	24	37	42	-2	10th
1920/21	(1)	42	9	8	4	31	25	6	6	9	28	38	44	-4	9th
1921/22	(1)	42	10	6	5	27	19	5	1	15	20	37	37	-9	17th
1922/23	(1)	42	13	4	4	38	16	3	6	12	23	46	42	-1	11th
1923/24	(1)	42	8	5	8	25	24	4	4	13	15	39	33	-23	19th
1924/25	(1)	42	12	3	6	33	17	2	2	17	13	41	33	-12	20th
1925/26	(1)	42	16	2	3	57	19	6	6	9	30	44	52	24	2nd
1926/27	(1)	42	12	5	4	47	30	5	4	12	30	56	43	-9	11th
1927/28	(1)	42	10	6	5	49	33	3	9	9	33	53	41	-4	10th
1928/29	(1)	42	11	6	4	43	25	5	7	9	34	47	45	5	9th
1929/30	(1)	42	10	2	9	49	26	4	9	8	29	40	39	12	14th
1930/31	(1)	42	14	5	2	67	27	14	5	2	60	32	66	68	1st(CH)
1931/32	(1)	42	14	5	2	52	16	8	5	8	38	32	54	42	2nd
1932/33	(1)	42	14	3	4	70	27	11	5	5	48	34	58	57	1st(CH)

| Season | Div | P | Home | | | | | Away | | | | | Pts | GD | Pos |
			W	D	L	F	A	W	D	L	F	A			
1933/34	(1)	42	15	4	2	45	19	10	5	6	30	28	59	28	1st(CH)
1934/35	(1)	42	15	4	2	74	17	8	8	5	41	29	58	69	1st(CH)
1935/36	(1)	42	9	9	3	44	22	6	6	9	34	26	45	30	6th
1936/37	(1)	42	10	10	1	43	20	8	6	7	37	29	52	31	3rd
1937/38	(1)	42	15	4	2	52	16	6	6	9	25	28	52	33	1st(CH)
1938/39	(1)	42	14	3	4	34	14	5	6	10	21	27	47	14	5th
						WORLD	WAR	II							
1946/47	(1)	42	9	5	7	43	33	7	4	10	29	37	41	2	13th
1947/48	(1)	42	15	3	3	56	15	8	10	3	25	17	59	49	1st(CH)
1948/49	(1)	42	13	5	3	51	18	5	8	8	23	26	49	30	5th
1949/50	(1)	42	12	4	5	48	24	7	7	7	31	31	49	24	6th
1950/51	(1)	42	11	5	5	47	28	8	4	9	26	28	47	17	5th
1951/52	(1)	42	13	7	1	54	30	8	4	9	26	31	53	19	3rd
1952/53	(1)	42	15	3	3	60	30	6	9	6	37	34	54	33	1st(CH)
1953/54	(1)	42	8	8	5	42	37	7	5	9	33	36	43	2	12th
1954/55	(1)	42	12	3	6	44	25	5	6	10	25	38	43	6	9th
1955/56	(1)	42	13	4	4	38	22	5	6	10	22	39	46	-1	5th
1956/57	(1)	42	12	5	4	45	21	9	3	9	40	48	50	16	5th
1957/58	(1)	42	10	4	7	48	39	6	3	12	25	46	39	-12	12th
1958/59	(1)	42	14	3	4	53	29	7	5	9	35	39	50	20	3rd
1959/60	(1)	42	9	5	7	39	38	6	4	11	29	42	39	-12	13th
1960/61	(1)	42	12	3	6	44	35	3	8	10	33	50	41	-8	11th
1961/62	(1)	42	9	6	6	39	31	7	5	9	32	41	43	-1	10th
1962/63	(1)	42	11	4	6	44	33	7	6	8	42	44	46	9	7th
1963/64	(1)	42	10	7	4	56	37	7	4	10	34	45	45	8	8th
1964/65	(1)	42	11	5	5	42	31	6	2	13	27	44	41	-6	13th
1965/66	(1)	42	8	8	5	36	31	4	5	12	26	44	37	-13	14th
1966/67	(1)	42	11	6	4	32	20	5	8	8	26	27	46	11	7th
1967/68	(1)	42	12	6	3	37	23	5	4	12	23	33	44	4	9th
1968/69	(1)	42	12	6	3	31	12	10	6	5	25	15	56	29	4th
1969/70	(1)	42	7	10	4	29	23	5	8	8	22	26	42	2	12th
1970/71	(1)	42	18	3	0	41	6	11	4	6	30	23	65	42	1st(CH)
1971/72	(1)	42	15	2	4	36	13	7	6	8	22	27	52	18	5th
1972/73	(1)	42	14	5	2	31	14	9	6	6	26	29	57	14	2nd
1973/74	(1)	42	9	7	5	23	16	5	7	9	26	35	42	-2	10th
1974/75	(1)	42	10	6	5	31	16	3	5	13	16	33	37	-2	16th
1975/76	(1)	42	11	4	6	33	19	2	6	13	14	34	36	-6	17th
1976/77	(1)	42	11	6	4	37	20	5	5	11	27	39	43	5	8th

Season	Div	P	Home W	D	L	F	A	Away W	D	L	F	A	Pts	GD	Pos
1977/78	(1)	42	14	5	2	38	12	7	5	9	22	25	52	23	5th
1978/79	(1)	42	11	8	2	37	18	6	6	9	24	30	48	13	7th
1979/80	(1)	42	8	10	3	24	12	10	6	5	28	24	52	16	4th
1980/81	(1)	42	13	8	0	36	17	6	7	8	25	28	53	16	3rd
1981/82	(1)	42	13	5	3	27	15	7	6	8	21	22	71	11	5th
1982/83	(1)	42	11	6	4	36	19	5	4	12	22	37	58	2	10th
1983/84	(1)	42	10	5	6	41	29	8	4	9	33	31	63	14	6th
1984/85	(1)	42	14	5	2	37	14	5	4	12	24	35	66	13	7th
1985/86	(1)	42	13	5	3	29	15	7	4	10	20	32	69	2	7th
1986/87	(1)	42	12	5	4	31	12	8	5	8	27	23	70	23	4th
1987/88	(1)	40	11	4	5	35	16	7	8	5	23	23	66	19	6th
1988/89	(1)	38	10	6	3	35	19	12	4	3	38	17	76	37	1st(CH)
1989/90	(1)	38	14	3	2	38	11	4	5	10	16	27	62	16	4th
1990/91	(1)	38	15	4	0	51	10	9	9	1	23	8	83*	56	1st(CH)
1991/92	(1)	42	12	7	2	51	23	7	8	6	30	24	72	35	4th
1992/93	(1)	42	8	6	7	25	20	7	5	9	15	18	56	2	10th
1993/94	(1)	42	10	8	3	25	15	8	9	4	28	13	71	30	4th
1994/95	(1)	42	6	9	6	27	21	7	3	11	26	28	51	3	12th
1995/96	(1)	38	10	7	2	30	16	7	5	7	19	16	63	17	5th
1996/97	(1)	38	10	5	4	36	18	9	6	4	26	14	68	30	3rd
1997/98	(1)	38	15	2	2	43	10	8	7	4	25	23	78	35	1st(CH)
1998/99	(1)	38	14	5	0	34	5	8	7	4	25	12	78	42	2nd
1999/2000	(1)	38	14	3	2	42	17	8	4	7	31	26	73	30	2nd
2000/01	(1)	38	15	3	1	45	13	5	7	7	18	25	70	30	2nd
2001/02	(1)	38	12	4	3	42	25	14	5	0	37	11	87	43	1st(CH)
2002/03	(1)	38	15	2	2	47	20	8	7	4	38	22	78	43	2nd
2003/04	(1)	38	15	4	0	40	14	11	8	0	33	12	90	47	1st(CH)
2004/05	(1)	38	13	5	1	54	19	12	3	4	33	17	83	51	2nd
2005/06	(1)	38	14	3	2	48	13	6	4	9	20	18	67	37	4th
2006/07	(1)	38	12	6	1	43	16	7	5	7	20	19	68	28	4th

*Two points deducted

CH = Champions
PR = Promoted
R = Relegated